Advance Praise

for The Joy Factor Recipe Book

"If you are passionately hungry for something different in your life, Wendy's book will give you just that. Her recipes, story and Joy Factor approach will be the perfect ingredients for anyone who wants to consciously create a life filled with more joy, passion and fulfillment. "

JANET BRAY ATTWOOD, *New York Times* Bestseller—Co-Author of *The Passion Test*

"Feeling good is a foundational piece of attracting what you want in life. Wendy shares valuable information that will help you to be happy and enjoy your journey."

BOB DOYLE, Author of *Wealth Beyond Reason* and *Follow Your Passion, Find Your Power: Everything You Need to Know about the Law of Attraction* and featured speaker on *The Secret*

"I highly recommend Wendy's take on how to create a joyful life; she demonstrates this so well in her book and models it for us in her life. This is the kind of real-life how to's that are vital to attract what you're craving."

JAN H. STRINGER, author of *BEE-ing Attraction and Attracting Perfect Customers*

"Anyone who meets Wendy would want to know her recipe for living joyfully. She seems to combine the ingredients so effortlessly. Her playful, practical book inspires us to apply attraction principles to manifest our desires. It's a delicious read."

TRICIA MOLLOY, Motivational Speaker and Author of *Divine Wisdom at Work: 10 Universal Principles for Enlightened Entrepreneurs*

"This book offers refreshingly simple ways for happiness to be more than something you wish for. Its unique recipes allow you to assemble the necessary ingredients for fulfillment. Once you have all the parts lined up, the only thing left is to put the icing on the cake—living a life of JOY!"

DR. LARRY MARKSON, Author of *Talking to Yourself is Not Crazy*

THE JOY

FACTOR
Recipe Book

A Common Sense Approach to a Delicious Life

Wendy Watkins, CPCC, PCC

First Edition 2012, Second Edition 2015

Cover Art and Interior Layout Design by: Vanessa Lowry
Editing by: Rebecca Ewing

This book may be purchased in bulk for educational, business, fundraising or sales promotional use. Special books or book excerpts can be created to fit specific needs. Contact the author at *www.wendywatkins.com*.

Library of Congress Control Number: 2012937452
ISBN: 978-1-61005-180-4

Printed in the United States of America by
BookLogix Publishing Services, Inc.

While the author has made every effort to provide accurate email and internet addresses at the time of publication, neither the author nor the publisher assume any responsibility for errors or for changes that occur after publication.

This book is dedicated to

Your Delicious Life

DISLCAIMER:

*The Joy Factor is a
coaching model that
takes you from where
you are to where
you want to go.
This is not a replacement
for therapy, counseling
or medication.
Use at your own risk—
the risk to live a more
joy-filled life!*

What's inside

Table of Contents

Thank You

To my wonderful husband Matt, who lovingly gave me space to write for two and a half years—you raise my Joy Factor. I love you.

To my sweet doggies Abbey Road and Eli, who were at my side consistently, with licks and tail wags.

To Vic, Aunt Nancy and Team Wendy: Bernadette, Kendra and Megha, who nurtured the seed of this book when it was just an idea.

To all of my parents, my sisters, in-laws, nieces and nephews; thank you for the unconditional love and encouragement.

To my Mastermind partner, Martha who cheered me on every Monday morning—gracias.

Thank you to every contributor in this book—my friends, clients and The Joy Posse.

Thank you to the artists that shared their vision of joy with their gorgeous pictures and illustrations.

Rebecca, my editor, Vanessa, my designer, and Booklogix, my publisher, made the journey oh so much easier.

I appreciate Erin, Victoria and Erin for their time and willingness to proof read my manuscript.

Thanks to Sally, Kim, Keith, Wanda and Michelle for opening up your homes so I could get away and write.

Thanks to my Creativity in Motion group, you showed up right on time.

To my neighbors, friends, colleagues and all of you that asked me, "How is the book coming?"

It is with joy and delight that I thank each and every one of you for seeing the possibility in me—I could not have completed this project without your support. Here is to joy for all!

Introduction

You are the chef of
your Joyful Life—now
is the perfect time to
create delectable days.

WENDY WATKINS

Introduction

*Change is
inevitable,
Ours is
incredible.*

So said a billboard about the renovation of a nearby apartment community. This statement is the essence of *The Joy Factor Recipe Book*. Change will happen, so why not deliberately make it appetizing?

After coaching hundreds of people through life and job transitions, leadership development and success planning, the common thread is: "How do I deal with so much change?" My clients also want to know how to make their transformation easier. I help them find their own answers and create a compelling plan. My own journey has been one of constant evolution. From paying attention to these quests, *The Joy Factor* blossomed.

Because of my deep love for both personal development and food, I bring them together to share this common-sense approach to having more joy in your life. From here, you can manifest the things, people and experiences that you desire and deserve. I use the word "recipe" to describe the instructions and guidelines that lead to sustainable happiness. Some you can prepare in your kitchen, but most are prepared in your heart, soul and conscious mind. All are delectable in their own way. Some are in story or essay form; others are actual exercises. Everything here is intended to evoke a feeling or connection to assist you in creating your personal recipe for joy.

Cooking a scrumptious meal takes time. Once you decide on the menu and gather the ingredients, the occasion has to be right. There have been more than a few vegetables thrown out because I thought I was going to make something, and didn't. The same rules apply to your happiness: select wisely and be patient. Let your process unfold like the ripening of summertime peach—the minute before it spoils is when it's most delicious.

After many years of searching for happiness from outside sources, I found it in the last place I thought to look, within myself. I often refer to the period of my life from the ages of thirteen to thirty-five as the "sex, drugs and rock n' roll era." In 2001, after reaching my limits of a life filled with lies, I ended my unhealthy relationship with drugs. This six-year process opened up new opportunities to create long-lasting pleasure on my own, while handling the cravings for all of the tempting, destructive things that still beckoned. This experience, combined with my thirty-plus-year study of personal development from Wayne Dyer, Louise Hay and Shakti Gawain (to name a few) and conversations with hundreds of my coaching clients, has prepared me to bring you this refreshing approach to finding happiness.

Whether you are new to the concepts of deliberately creating your life, or you're eager to move from "talking the talk" to "walking the walk," this book gives you a crisp interpretation of this essential wisdom. The concepts are not new, yet they are shared in a refreshing way, like cold lemonade on a hot summer day.

The beginning chapters explain *The Joy Factor*, followed by a short quiz to determine which ingredients to use to cook up your good life. The next chapter gives an overview of your utensils. The premise of this book is that you are a conscious creator—the chef of your life—using these ingredients:

Connection to Passion

Authentic Expression

Self-Care

Strategic Optimism

After reading recipes and stories written by others like you, each on a quest for more happiness, you'll easily be able to create your own recipe.

Julia Child's legacy is about great cooking. At thirty-seven years old, she was still discovering who she was. In *My Life in France* she shares "...no one is born a great cook, one learns by doing." Whether you are twenty-seven, seventy-seven or somewhere in between, now is the perfect time to create delectable days. You'll reap many benefits, but mostly, you will be happy. From there, amazing things will unfold.

Cheers to your delicious life.

*Cheers to your
delicious life.*

Chapter 1

Food
for
Thought

When you align with your Joy Factor you will learn to enjoy your life, even when it's different than you expected.

WENDY WATKINS

Chapter 1

Food for Thought

Joy is finding a pair of comfy, cute shoes, in my size, on the clearance rack. Or sharing a delicious meal with a favorite friend. Better still if I can show her my new shoes. Later, though, there are those gorgeous boots on my wish list, and I am hungry again. The treats have come and gone.

In contrast, The Joy Factor produces *sustainable* happiness that sticks around after the brownie has been devoured and the shoes have worn out. This is the key to the eternal grin. It's what keeps us feeling good and focused, attracting more and more of what we really want.

There are two women I regularly see at the gym. Every time, they have ready smiles and something nice to say. They exude delight, and are surrounded by people talking, laughing, and smiling. Their magnetic energy does not wane, for it has nothing to do with their cars, gym clothes, jewelry or status. It has everything to do with who and what they have chosen to be. It has become a part of their identities.

"When we are centered in joy, we attain our wisdom."
– MARIANNE WILLIAMSON

The ingredients for the Joy Factor can be compared to sugar, eggs, milk, flour and butter. With these five ingredients, you can get custard or cake. How you combine them, and in what proportion, are in direct relation to the results you crave. You may want a healthful cake, so you find ingredients that are wholesome. If the ingredients are pure and you put in the amounts that are right for you, the recipe will always work.

The same is true for combining the ingredients that will raise your Joy Factor. Authentic Expression, Connection to your Passions, Self-Care and Strategic Optimism can be mixed up in countless ways. Working with these will make your life so delicious that you'll want to lick the bowl and the spoon. You'll savor your unique definition of joy.

Trish Carr, a twenty-plus-year girlfriend and joy enthusiast, shares this distinction between happiness and joy.

Happy, Happy, Joy, Joy

Joy. I love that feeling. "Joy" goes beyond "Happy." Even dictionary.com agrees:

"Happy" means:

1. *delighted, pleased, or glad, as over a particular thing.*
2. *characterized by or indicative of pleasure, contentment.*

To me that sounds like "Fine," "OK" or "Good."

Whereas "Joy" is defined as:

1. *the emotion of great delight caused by something exceptionally good or satisfying.*
2. *keen pleasure; elation.*

How would you rather feel—pleased or elated? I'm thinking "elated" wins hands down. When I feel elated there is a fullness in my body, almost like there's so much inside I'm going to burst. It feels like...Thankfulness. It feels like...Power. It feels like...Love. What does Joy feel like for you?

My life, like yours, has many distractions. Emails to answer, more phone calls to return than time, and more projects than can possibly be managed effectively. Yet when I remind myself to find Joy in the moment, I see it everywhere: In my four-year old nephew's laughter, in my husband's touch, in the rich flavor of my coffee.

When you stop and notice you'll see the joy in your life. You'll hear and feel it in the rustle of the trees on a breezy summer day; in the symphony of the birds singing; in the expressive faces of children and in the kiss from your romantic partner; the rich conversations with your friends; in the beautiful color of your eyes; in how amazing you look in that dress. Delight is there, you just have to become aware of it.

When I am cheerful, things seem to go more smoothly, people are nicer and I accomplish more in my day. Like most things in life, Joy is a choice. In any situation, at any time, I can choose to find what's good. So why not go further than finding the good and find the Joy? I can be pleased or glad in any situation, or I can choose to feel great delight, even elated. It's my decision. When I feel Joy, absolutely nothing can stop me from living a magical life.

Fill in the blank space with your definition of joy.

_____

_____

_____

_____

_____

{ • } { • } { • }

At the grocery store recently, there was an adorable but cranky little girl throwing a fit because she wanted Lucky Charms. NOW. If her mother did not put it in the buggy immediately, it would be the end of her sweet little world. I can still hear her demanding, "Now Mommy!"

Our society seems to thrive on instant gratification. We want that car, house, cereal, etc. NOW! The price for "NOW" has been steep for some. The Joy Factor approach is based on a similar principle: you can experience joy now, without any fallout, debt or extra storage space, or when the outcome is not what you planned.

An experience of making the most out of a situation happened the day we drove for nearly an hour to watch the sunset from the beach. I just knew it was going to be a glorious sight. We spread our blanket and relaxed. The sun disappeared into the horizon and to my surprise, there was merely an inkling of color. Hmph. Not what we expected, so we sat back and listened: the soft roar of the surf, the laughter of children playing and dogs barking close by shifted our senses to the nuance of sound; a chorus of life, pleasure and movement. It was beautiful.

It is our right to feel good, to be happy. Yes, there is an ebb and flow to the tide, and the sun rises and sets. Life cycles are inevitable. Some even believe that our capacity for joy is proportional to our experience of sorrow. But this I know is true: when we embrace this rhythmic cycle and make conscious choices, we will taste the long-term delight. When you align with your Joy Factor you will learn to enjoy your life, even when it's different than you expected.

The four ingredients of The Joy Factor provide a foundation for you to have more and more of what you desire and deserve. Doesn't that sound as delicious as warm chocolate chip cookies and cold milk? Or for you that may be chips and dip. You get to choose.

Deb Cooperman, one of my first coaches and part of the Joy Posse on my Joy Factor blog is a writing evangelist, writing coach and workshop leader. She loves to coach writers and creative people. Enjoy her perspective on joy.

It's a Beautiful Day....in the hospital

In the spring of 2009, I had big-time surgery. When I awoke and learned that I didn't have cancer—as my doctor thought I did (yee ha!)—the recovery, even with several bumps in the road, became a great opportunity to practice joy.

Getting up and walking around the day after having my belly sliced was a requirement for healing, but it wasn't easy. Somehow, re-writing the lyrics to Diana Ross' "I'm Coming Out" and singing them each time I did helped. "I'm getting ... up. I'm inching off the bed, shufflin' cross the floor ..." Eating the pudding they served with lunch did too. (Hospital food is notoriously bad, but pudding is almost always good.)

A few days after being discharged, I was back in the emergency room with a high fever and an infection. My sister went with me, and as we waited for tests, and then for the results—dragging on until the wee hours of the morning—she took photos of us on her cell phone commemorating the adventure. One of the residents looked in on us as we giggled and said, "You are far too upbeat for someone with a 102-degree fever." "Doc," I replied, "I don't have cancer. This is nothing."

Later, waiting on a gurney in a hallway for an MRI, I heard U2's "Beautiful Day" pumping out of a radiologists office and bobbed my head in a makeshift dance. The attendant gave me a quizzical look as he came to wheel me into the room. "Dancing?" he laughed. "How can you resist this song?" I asked. He slowed down, listened and said, "Yeah, I guess it is a beautiful day."

I wound up being admitted for three more days to fight the infection, but friends brought magazines, I listened to plenty of great music on my iPod, wrote out my gratitude in my journal, and ate plenty of pudding.

Surgery isn't fun, nor is fever or an infection. And joy might have eluded me (for a while, anyway) had the *outcome been different, but I saw clearly that when life gets tough, being goofy, upbeat and joy-filled really **can** be the sugar that makes the medicine go down.*

This approach is for anyone who is ready to consciously create a life of joy. No more creating by default or accepting whatever lands in your lap. Albert Einstein defined insanity as "doing the same thing again and again and expecting different results." In order to make shifts to take you down an innovative path, stop whining and complaining about why you cannot achieve your desire and spend that same energy doing something different. Oprah knows this for sure, "Worrying is wasted time. Use the same energy for doing something about whatever worries you."

I have a secret: my beautiful red hair is not really mine, except that I paid for it, so I do own it. Getting my hair colored is the only quick fix I know that works, even though I only get six weeks of grey coverage—I mean joy—from it. Sustainable satisfaction comes from making small changes on a consistent basis. It is about waking up and being conscious of the choices you make each and every day. Begin with acknowledging your successes and adjust what is not working so you get more of what you fancy. It could be an overall enjoyment, or it could be targeted towards specific areas of your life like relationships, career, family, health or finances. Just decide what you want and take steps to deliberately create it! I know that every six weeks I will need to spend time with my hairdresser again to have her bring me back to my desired color. Joy!

Joy is the best make-up.

ANNE LAMOTT

When I arrived in Atlanta twenty-four years ago, I had to learn to maneuver the still-dreaded loop that encircles greater Atlanta: Interstate 285. One of the Atlanta Braves missed a game once because he got on I-285 and didn't know where to get off. It goes round and round. One minute you are going to the east and the next minute you are going south. It is very confusing to me. If I don't plan in advance, I frantically call my husband to ask which exit to take. It doesn't feel good to be unsure of where I am going.

Think of how many people you know who are bouncing around their life, unsure of their direction. If you do not know where you are heading, you will never get there. The same goes for joy and happiness. If you are not consciously creating it, you will forfeit too much of it. It is a false truth that you can achieve the heights of sustainable joy with outside substitutes. It will be good for a minute before becoming more of the same results that you do not love. I say, pick something else.

ART BY KENDRA ARMACOST

Holocaust survivor, writer and neurologist Viktor Frankl tapped an inner core of strength and wisdom to transmute his incarceration in a Nazi concentration camp. Even in the absolute worst-of-the-worst conditions, he found the ability to survive and thrive, and his contribution to the fields of psychology and psychiatry has influenced healing ever since. Your freedom lies in your hands, your heart and your mind. Once you grasp the truth of your situation, you can find the information, people and resources to build on your new-found freedom and truth.

The strength and knowledge to change your life is inside of you, and you don't have to hit "rock bottom" to find it. You can if you want to, but it isn't necessary. You need only to stop long enough to reconnect with your authentic inner self, and listen to that voice. Once you do, you'll find story after story of courageous people who created a new and better situation for themselves. As the age-old idiom urged, they made lemonade from their lemons, and found it tasty.

THE INGREDIENTS

Here is a taste of the distinctive ingredients that will raise your Joy Factor. These components for bliss are no longer hush-hush. They are ripe and ready to use to enhance this one-time appearance you have here in this body. Relish the essence of each one and notice what you notice.

AUTHENTIC EXPRESSION

This ingredient is about being you. There is nothing as sweet as being able to show up one hundred percent yourself in each and every situation. Let's start with a poem and explore this ingredient from there.

Nobody Does it Better

BY FRAN ASARO

When you look into the mirror
When you look outside the box
When you peek into the depths of you
That's when opportunity knocks
You bring this world a value
That to others will attach
You have that way about you
That no one else can match
Continuing to learn from others
On top of each other we are built
We all bring an attribute
That creates a patchwork quilt
None of this could happen
Should you refuse to play along
Your participation is required
To launch this universal song
Nobody does it better
That thing there that you do
So bring it to the table
To share the gift of you.

Fran is a coach and woman on a mission to help others flourish. When I met Fran, her commitment to people being their best self confirmed my inkling that she had to be part of this joy movement.

*In becoming
fully human,
we are called to
be individuals.
We are called to be
unique and different.*

M. SCOTT PECK

The more you give yourself permission to be you and share that self with the world, the easier it will be to raise your Joy Factor. It is not always effortless to express a genuine appearance of yourself. Singer and songwriter Dave Matthews song, "So Much to Say," reminds me that when you use this delicious ingredient, it becomes easier and more natural to be yourself. The result? More joy! Do you think it was easy for Oprah to express her true nature in the early years? She took mindful steps to be her best each and every day. The same is true for you. As you uncover and allow your true being to come out, the strewn puzzle pieces will fall into place. You'll feel secure in expressing your thoughts and feelings, as well as your dreams, desires and opinions. It will open up doors that you may have never dreamed possible.

After many years of running successful cleaning businesses and founding the professional non-profit association for his industry, my client, Perry, still felt something was not right. There was something more he wanted to be doing—bigger gifts he was meant to share with the world, yet he didn't know what. He enjoyed writing, connecting people, and sharing resources that helped his colleagues to be more successful. As he continued to build the next iteration of his cleaning business he stopped, listened, and watched for signs. He began a trade publication to serve his industry. Suddenly his "alive-o-meter" cranked up. Writing articles and collaborating with writers really lit him up. He responded to his craving for enhanced communication in his field and found the medium that felt right. The beauty of Perry's story is that as he gained clarity and used the power of authentic expression to raise his Joy Factor, he was creating a life he loved. He did not get stuck in the *hows*. As a conscious creator, Perry was clear on *what* it was he wanted to create and the *hows* made themselves clear. He kept putting one foot in front of the other, moving toward his desire of expressing himself in a way that felt good and making the positive impact he wanted in the world. He'll be the first to tell you that his journey was not always easy. However, he was compelled to move forward because the excitement, optimism, gratitude and contentment he experienced were, simply, too joyful to ignore.

> ### *"I define joy as a sustained sense of well-being and internal peace—a connection to what matters."*
> – OPRAH WINFREY

What could Authentic Expression do for your life? Would it free you from pretending? This is the time to be you and feel good about it. A revered teacher of mine reminded me that it is none of my business what other people think about me. This mantra reminds me that as long as I am being honest and true to myself, and not intentionally hurting anyone in the process, I can move forward in creating a life that I love.

CONNECTION TO PASSION

People come into our lives for many reasons. My friend, Bernadette Peters, is here to share her carefree spirit, infectious laugh and deep wisdom with friends for the sake of increased joy. This is what she notices about passion.

Finding Joy in the Moment

Barry owns "The Filling Station" deli down the street. He makes a mean Cuban and my favorite egg salad and bacon sandwich. Most of the conversations we have are short and on the run, because as a hard worker, his small business encompasses most of his life.

One morning, Barry came into our coffee shop before we opened, and we had a slightly longer conversation. Barry was lit up, even before having his caffeine. That weekend he had expressed his creativity and passion by catering a nice dinner for a couple celebrating their anniversary.

Barry talked about the special menu requests from his client, the way he set the table and readied the meal, leaving the couple to be alone and enjoy their wonderful date. He described how the wife looked at her husband. That warmed his heart and fed his spirit.

It was fun to see the enthusiasm on Barry's face and hear such passion in his words—all because he was able to express his creativity. If we all did that from time to time, our joy would make a positive impact on the world.

Do you express your creativity through painting, song, writing, problem-solving, gardening or a wonderful meal? Figure out what lights your fire like Barry, and be sure to make time to do it.

Fill in the blank space with what lights your fire.

_____

_____

The only true measure of success is the amount of joy we are feeling.

ABRAHAM-HICKS

Passion adds zest and meaning to your days; it is a spice of life. Imagine a world where everyone knew what they were truly passionate about and designed their life around that. There would be more joy and less depression, more celebration and fewer addictions. Napoleon Hill touches on the importance of Connection to Passion when he speaks about knowing what your "burning desire" is in the book, *Think and Grow Rich*. This success principle was introduced at the turn of the twentieth century and helped produce achievement for many people. Being a conscious creator is about knowing what form you want your life to take. As it takes shape and you stay linked to your desire, your "Big Why," then the joy really expands. We're still benefiting from this information one hundred years later. As you experience your Passion, you will connect to more success and fulfillment.

Martha has been my mastermind partner for over three years. She is a videographer who creates amazing videos that are beautiful and informative. For many years, she served non-profits and educated the Hispanic community in South Florida about AIDS. She was extremely successful and mildly happy. She knew there was something more for her. After connecting with a new teacher and uncovering a passion for real estate, she understood how to create a win-win situation for herself and others. She is improving low-income tenants' quality of life, while building her financial future. This will allow her to enjoy an earlier retirement, focus on her spiritual community, and pay it forward to the Hispanic community while enjoying her journey!

Bob Doyle, author of *Wealth Beyond Reason* and *Follow Your Passion, Find Your Power: Everything You Need to Know about the Law of Attraction* has this to say about passion:

"There are so many reasons that it is true, when we are living a life aligned with our passions and inspired action, including the sense of accomplishment we feel when we're up to something big. People are more joyful when they contribute something; that indescribable feeling when they're in a state of bliss from doing something they truly love. They are contributing greatly to their own lives, and serving as an inspiration for others."

SELF-CARE

Trish Carr supports women world-wide as the co-founder of Women's Prosperity Network, the premiere organization for professional and personal development for today's woman. She shares this delightful morsel about her version of Self-Care.

The Joy in Dieting...Really...

*I love to eat. That **Eat, Pray, Love** lady has nothing on me. I can eat with the best of them and I don't have to go to Italy to do it. I've always been one of those people that "lives to eat," rather than, "eats to live." I know people like that, eating simply to live, they actually forget to eat. Can you imagine? Forgetting to eat? I don't know about you but at breakfast I'm planning lunch...and usually dinner, too.*

I've been on a weight loss program where I eat only one meal a day and replace the other two with nutritional shakes. I've never been a meal replacement fan, I always preferred to eat my calories rather than drink them—unless you're talking "adult beverages." But this time I needed a good jump-start so I tried it. And I'm glad I finally gave in and did. The shakes, which on day one tasted barely palatable, today taste like Dairy Queen! It's amazing what we can train ourselves to believe. Talk about being joyful! I get Dairy Queen for breakfast every day!

And my meal, my one meal a day, is the best food I've ever eaten. Really. The BEST food I've ever eaten. Since I'm only getting one meal, I'm making it myself and I'm making it like Martha Stewart would—cloth napkins, fine china, beautifully plated colorful organic veggies, scrumptious grilled fish, and a bountiful green salad.

Another side benefit, my taste-buds have experienced a re-birth. For the first time in a long time, I not only can taste the food I eat, I know what "satisfied" feels like. And it doesn't take as much food as I thought it did. So I'm doing great, losing weight, feeling energetic, exercising and enjoying the ride. Will someone please remind me of this when the holidays are here?

As the components of this ingredient are revealed, you will uncover a type of Self-Care that really works for you. If you are someone who is not familiar with taking care of yourself, this concept may feel very uncomfortable at first. It may feel more like selfishness. The difference is that self-centeredness is based on the principle that you do not care about anyone else but yourself. Self-Care is the exact opposite. You care so much about others that you will take care of yourself to be the best you can for them and for yourself. It is a win-win. However, when you do anything new, it usually feels strange, right?

TRY THIS: take your hands, put them together and let your fingers intertwine. Notice how that feels. Now, undo them and intertwine them with the opposite thumb on top. Now, notice how that feels.

Self-Care may feel a bit strange at first, just like having your non-dominant thumb on top. The more you practice this act of self-love, it becomes familiar and comfortable. You'll wonder why it took so long to care for yourself. Your version of Self-Care may or may not look like what your sister, mother, colleague or partner is doing for themselves. You may learn a thing or two from their practices; however, this is about what you want to do for you to feel good. What will nurture your spirit?

The first thirty minutes of every day is a gift I give to myself. In the early morning hours, I shuffle upstairs with my steaming cup of joe and savor the silence. After sitting quietly for fifteen minutes or so, I write. I may pick a card or two or three from one of my many inspirational card decks or just lie on the floor and pet my sweet sleepy doggies. The intention of my morning ritual is to ease into the day with peace, joy and love. This sets me up to be the best I can be for myself, my family, my clients and the people who want to merge into my lane of traffic at the very last minute.

Whether it is rituals, taking a walk, eating wholesome foods or singing in the shower, Self-Care is a vital item to have in your recipe. Once you find a flavor you like, it will be easy to enjoy it on a daily basis.

The secret to achieve true success is found in your daily routine.

AUTHOR UNKNOWN

STRATEGIC OPTIMISM

A young boy, dealing with family challenges, has a life-altering idea when his social studies teacher gives them this intriguing assignment: think of something to change the world and put it into action. Even if you did not see the film, you have probably heard of the concept—Pay it Forward. Trevor McKinney decided that instead of repaying good deeds with payback, he would do three good deeds for three new people. This revolutionary idea enhanced his life as well as those around him.

The ability to plan for optimism; to believe, expect and hope that things will turn out for the best shines a bright light on your day-to-day existence. As you embrace the attitude of someone who feels positive and confident, a world of possibilities open up. As you learn to create a strategy—a carefully devised plan of action to achieve your goal of optimism, so many pieces of your conscious-creation puzzle will fall into place. Whether your plan includes practicing random acts of kindness or spending more time with uplifting people, this ingredient can quickly bring contentment your way. It can be as simple as how you choose to look at your world.

Tricia Molloy, author of *Divine Wisdom at Work: 10 Universal Principles for Enlightened Entreprenuers*, shares this:

"Strategic Optimism is a good way to say that I look at every opportunity as a positive one. When I am faced with disappointment or a setback, I tend to look at it as something better must be coming my way. This keeps my vibration up to allow more positivity to come into my life."

Each of these ingredients will add something special to your life. When you combine them, you create the award-winning recipe called, "I Love My Life!" It will give you something to infuse into your body besides substances, thoughts and things that are not serving you in living your most delicious life.

Are you ready to shift and are not sure how? Here is a splendid recipe gathered from a request to my friends on Facebook. It's a delicious collaboration for you to enjoy.

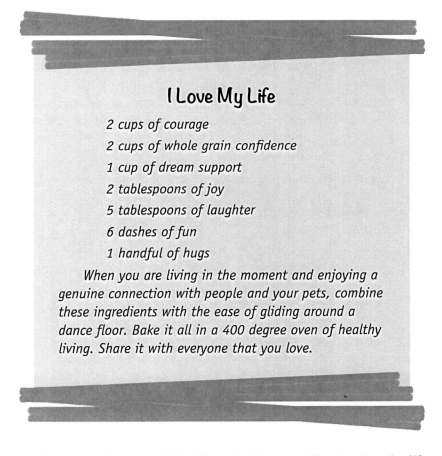

I Love My Life

2 cups of courage

2 cups of whole grain confidence

1 cup of dream support

2 tablespoons of joy

5 tablespoons of laughter

6 dashes of fun

1 handful of hugs

When you are living in the moment and enjoying a genuine connection with people and your pets, combine these ingredients with the ease of gliding around a dance floor. Bake it all in a 400 degree oven of healthy living. Share it with everyone that you love.

More days than not, I feel like pinching myself as I enjoy the life that I've made from these four straight-forward ingredients:

Connection to my Passion,
Authentic Expression,
Strategic Optimism
and Self-Care.

Experienced people say that everything that has happened in their life, good or bad, has made them the person that they are today. Each and every ingredient in their recipe is part of their unique combination. The same is true for you. You may have tried these ingredients in the past and they didn't work or you may have heard of them yet been afraid to taste them. Twenty years ago, raw fish was disgusting to me; I did not know the right way to enjoy this delicacy. Now I cannot get enough sushi.

The late Edwin Neill, a beloved mentor, often quoted Mark Twain: "If you always do what you have always done, you will always get what you always got." What ingredients do you want to use to get something different in your life?

It is time for you to create your Joy Factor shopping list. With this philosophy, it is important to know which ingredients you already have and what you may need to discard, so you can consciously decide for what you need to "go shopping."

Chapter 2

What
is in
Your Pantry?

ART BY EVELYN BALLIN

Chapter 2

What is in *Your* Pantry?

n the days of Shakespeare, feedback was immediate, and sometimes smelly. When the audience disapproved of the acting on stage, they booed and hissed freely. If they really objected, they hurled rotten tomatoes at the actors.

Are there spoiled ingredients in your recipe? Maybe you are dependent on external substances to bring you happiness, such as food, alcohol, shopping or drugs. Perhaps your substance of choice is negative self-talk or fear of change. Since these don't have the texture or smell of moldy vegetables, and no one (besides yourself) is tossing them at you, you may not know just what is rotten.

A few years ago, I had reached my highest weight ever and I didn't feel comfortable in my body. I ranted to anyone who would listen, "I feel fat." My repetitive story was boring and the ending was always the same: feeling too large. After working with my coach, and reminding myself of the teachings I share with others, I opted to love my body regardless of its size. This first step led me to modify my food selection, and to participate in activities that nurtured my body and spirit, and the pounds began to melt off. It was not a painless process, yet it was better than being saddled each day with sadness, shame and regret; I was able to enjoy food without it being my main source of (pseudo) happiness. At snack time these days, I do my best to remember to ask, "What am I really feeding here?" When I am nourishing a true hunger, rather than an emotional need, I avoid reverting to my state of woe.

*We are new
every day.*

IRENE CLAREMONT DE CASTILLEGO

Do you have a rut like mine? Most of us do. Think about an area in your life where you feel stuck. The Universal Law of Attraction states that wherever you put your energy, thoughts and focus, whether you want it or not, you attract more of that into your life. To slowly but surely change your hunger, shift your attention to what will nurture you. Instead of thinking about eating fewer cookies, I focused on adding more green vegetables and water. Placing attention on what you want versus what you don't want will help nudge you out of your rut.

My friend Jackie was constantly complaining about her job. She was an expert in her field of choice, and money came easily to her, but not contentment. She rarely enjoyed the lifestyle she could. She was stuck in her rut and thought everyone lived this way, settling for what they had, and suffering through it. She found her path to pleasure by reflecting on happier days. She recalled feeling freedom when she tapped into her creativity, and began to weave this familiar, exuberant energy into her everyday life. She started taking photographs again and eventually, showed her work at local galleries.

She remained in her job, with a fresh perspective. Altering her focus transformed her existence and changed her world.

IT IS TIME TO CHANGE YOUR WORLD.

We'll use The Joy Factor Quiz to see how much of each ingredient is currently in your cupboard. Pick the answer that best reflects you most of the time.

You will score this quiz in two ways:

- At the end of each section, you will see how much of this ingredient you need in your personal recipe for joy and fulfillment.
- At the end of the quiz, you can total your four scores to see where your Joy Factor is today.

PASSION

1. How clear are you about your passions?
    A. I am very clear and passion is present in most areas of my life.
    B. I am somewhat clear and some of my passions are present in my life.
    C. I am unclear. My passions are nowhere to be found.

2. If you had a magic wand and could change your life in any way that you wanted to, would you make a lot of changes?
    A. I would make very few changes.
    B. There are a few areas that I would like to enhance.
    C. I would buy extra batteries to make sure my magic wand could handle all of the changes.

3. Do you tend to make decisions from your head or your heart?
    A. There is a perfect combination available for me to make decisions in my life.
    B. I make most decisions with my head, but am listening more often to my heart.
    C. All head, no heart.

4. When you have clarity about the path you want to be on, do you move forward with ease?
    A. I am clear and connected; I move forward with ease.
    B. I do a cha cha—2 steps forward, 1 step back, pause, pause.
    C. It is challenging for me to get into action.

5. How connected are you to your "Big Why"?

    A. I am clear and connected.

    B. I am somewhat clear, and somewhat connected.

    C. Unclear and disconnected.

Passion Results: A=3   B=2   C=1

15-13 points: You experience a good connection with your passions. They will always be a good flavor enhancer for you.

12-9 points: A bit more passion would improve your recipe.

8 and below: Add more passion liberally to your recipe for a scrumptious life.

Recipes for the Passion ingredient can be found in Chapter Four.

AUTHENTIC EXPRESSION

6. How often do you do and say what you want to do and say?

    A. I say and do what I feel most of the time.

    B. There are times that I worry about what others think, so I censor myself.

    C. I rarely reveal what I really feel.

7. How comfortable are you in your own skin?

    A. Most of the time I love who I am.

    B. I am conscious of what I want to change and am working on it.

    C. I often wish I was somebody else.

8. How supportive is your self-talk?

    A. My champion voice is mostly present every day.

    B. Somewhat supportive, but there is a continual dialogue between my champion and inner critic.

    C. It is more detrimental than supportive.

9. If your life were made into a movie, what type of award would it receive?

    A. Best Picture of the Decade

    B. Best Director, yet the acting is not so good.

    C. Not even nominated.

10. Think about what you currently do for a living. Is it what you want to be doing or are you doing it because you think you should or have to?

    A. I love my job/career and wouldn't change it for the world.

    B. I enjoy my job most of the time, yet wonder about other things.

    C. Are you hiring?

Authentic Expression Results: A=3   B=2   C=1

15-13 points: You express yourself beautifully. Keep it up and add in other layers of Authentic Expression as needed.

12-9 points: You are comfortable in sharing your authentic self most of the time.

8 and below: Authentic Expression would enhance your recipe today.

Recipes for the Authentic Expression ingredient can be found in Chapter Five.

SELF-CARE

11. When you look at your life thus far, would you say you have been more loyal to your own needs or to the needs of others?

    A. I consciously take care of my needs first, so I can take care of others.

    B. There is a so-so mixture of attention on myself and others.

    C. It is always about everyone else.

12. When you think about your health, are you happy with how you take care of your body?

    A. I am very pleased with the choices I make to support my health.

    B. Most of the time; yet I wish I could be more consistent with my intentions.

    C. I don't pay much attention and I'm not pleased with what I see or feel.

13. Most people are looking to live a life of balance. What is balance like for you today?

    A. I feel quite balanced most of the time.

    B. I wobble on the teeter-totter of life.

    C. I am off-balance today.

14. Imagine that your mind is a funnel to feeling good. Are you putting in good things or not-so-good things?

    A. I am conscious of what I read, watch, and with whom I spend my time.

B. I am mostly aware, yet know that I sometimes feed my mind garbage.

C. Lots of rubbish.

15. Feelings are an intricate part of our lives. How connected are you to what you are feeling?

A. I am connected and aware of my feelings, and act accordingly.

B. I am somewhat connected, yet sometimes forget to pay attention to them.

C. What are feelings? I am numb.

Self Care Results: A=3   B=2   C=1

15-13 points: You are taking good care of yourself and it shows. Keep adding this ingredient as needed for flavor.

12-9 points: A tad more Self Care would perk up your recipe.

8 and below: Self Care belongs in your pantry. Select what works for you and pick some up today.

Recipes for the Self Care ingredient can be found in Chapter Six.

STRATEGIC OPTIMISM

16. How easily are you able to "enjoy the journey"?

A. The journey is the best part—I look forward to it and I adjust when I veer off course.

B. I enjoy it most of the time, yet sometimes I have to stop and remind myself.

C. The journey is not very fun. Are we there yet?

17. What type of plan do you have for your life?
    A. I have a clear vision of what I want and am on the path to creating it.
    B. The plan has lots of things crossed out and penciled in; I am working on it.
    C. What plan?

18. Do you appreciate what you have in life?
    A. I am very happy with all that I have and acknowledge it regularly.
    B. I am somewhat content.
    C. No.

19. Is the glass half full or half empty?
    A. My glass is overflowing.
    B. Usually half full, yet sometimes needs a refill.
    C. Dry as a bone.

20. In your relationships, do you think more about what you can do for others, or what they can do for you?
    A. I love to be able to support others.
    B. Most of the time is spent on what I can do for them, with some time spent wondering what they will do for me.
    C. What have you done for me lately?

Strategic Optimism Results: A=3   B=2   C=1

15-13 points: Your glass is very full. Keep up whatever you are doing.

12-9 points: Add a smidgen more of this ingredient and you will savor every bite.

8 and below: Strategic Optimism will add a tremendous amount of zest to your life.

Recipes for the Strategic Optimism ingredient can be found in Chapter Seven.

TOTAL ALL OF YOUR INGREDIENTS:

60-47: Your Joy Factor ingredients support you in creating a life that you love.

46-34: Your Joy Factor is yearning for more attention from you.

33 and below: You can increase your Joy Factor today.

    If this quiz proved how wisely you are using your ingredients, BRAVO—your life is pretty delicious. If your recipe needs something more, or your cupboard is bare, the following chapters will show you how to cook up something wonderful.

    Each chapter offers "recipes" to use in your cookbook of life experiences. These innovative recipes include a unique and inspiring combination of stories, rituals, exercises, and tidbits of information to help you learn and grow.

    For example, enjoy this recipe with your morning beverage from my friend, client, and life coach, Carolyn Jones.

A Simple Recipe for Creating a Perfect Day

2 heaping cups of Gratitude

1 cup of Intentions

1/2 cup of Centering

Begin with Gratitude every morning, add in Intentions, and stir gently until Centered.

The real issue is not whether to grow, it is how to grow and for what purpose.

ANONYMOUS

If any recipe tastes good, use it again and again. There are plenty of pages for you to write your own sumptuous instructions later in the book.

Here is another story from Bernadette. She and her partner Pat increased my Joy Factor by introducing me to cycling, which was not always comfortable in those early days.

PHOTO BY PAT THOMAS

Pushing through Uncomfortable to Greater Joy

The other night I went to what I call "Jersey Yoga." It's a bit of a tough class, and I always walk away with something valuable. I love Renee, the instructor and my friend. She is extremely flexible, unlike me, and a teacher at heart. Teaching yoga comes easily to her and brings her happiness.

She started class with thoughts about doing things that don't come naturally. For the past ten years, Renee has carried her guitar with her, yearning to play. She is uncomfortable with the upstroke—it is awkward for her and makes her want to stop trying. She kept at it, making a small adjustment to how she was holding the guitar, allowing the upstroke to flow comfortably and create the nice sound she wanted. Pressing on led to a small breakthrough that gave her great joy on her musical journey.

During the class, she challenged us to be self-teachers, doing things that might be uncomfortable for the possibility of that joyful breakthrough. I made small adjustments, experimenting and discovering how this old stiff body could do more. It was inspirational to watch two other students practice forearm stands, making the shifts that allowed them to do this for the first time. It gave them a big sense of accomplishment.

Keep doing what comes naturally and you'll certainly find happiness, but if you push through something uncomfortable, you will experience a deeper sense of joy.

Knowing the ingredients you need to raise your Joy Factor is just the beginning. Now it's time to change things up a little.

My husband Matt loves to cook (How lucky am I?). When he tells me dinner will be ready in thirty minutes, I know that it will really be forty-five minutes to an hour and I plan accordingly. The same is true for your recipes. They may take a minute, a day, or a year longer to fully prepare than you thought they would. Stick with it. Your delicious life is worth the wait.

You don't have to wait for one of my favorite recipes from Matt. Gather the ingredients for this vegetarian chili; you will be glad you did.

Matt's Veggie Chili

1 large onion, diced

2 Tablespoons cumin—if he measured,
   this is what it would be

1 Tablespoon chili powder

3 Chipotle peppers in adobo sauce, chopped

1 28-ounce can of fire-roasted tomatoes

5 cans of assorted beans (make sure one
   of them is Garbanzo beans)

1 block of firm tofu, drained and cubed

1 pound of frozen corn

Sauté onions with cumin, chili powder and chipotles
in large pot. Add everything else, except the corn and
simmer at least thirty minutes. Add corn ten minutes
before serving. Garnish with cheese, sour cream and of
course, joy.

"Move out of your comfort zone.
You can only grow if you are willing to feel awkward
and uncomfortable when you try something new."
– BRIAN TRACY

Chapter 3

Flavor
Enhancers

Every day you choose
what "glasses" to wear
and they affect how
you see the world.

WENDY WATKINS

Chapter 3

Flavor Enhancers

Traditional cookbooks often share resources about cooking utensils to craft the delectable dishes featured in the book. In this nontraditional recipe book, you'll get supplementary information about tools to cook up a life of joy that include, yet are not limited to, the Universal Laws of Attraction, Conscious Creation, and Inspired Action. These philosophies blend beautifully with Passion, Authentic Expression, Self-Care and Strategic Optimism; the Joy Factor ingredients that you'll use in your personal recipe.

During my professional coach training in 2000, I took a course called Fulfillment. I hoped it would satisfy my craving for more satisfaction and success. One of the best morsels in that class was receiving my "MSU." This makeshift qualification was more relevant than any diploma I have received. From that day on, I use my MSU regularly to "Make Stuff Up." Ponder this concept: you make up every thought you think. Whatever you are thinking now about the concept of an MSU, you are creating. When used correctly, it will satisfy your cravings and transform your life. Congratulations! You can now use your own MSU to create a life you adore.

On my drive to the gym each morning, traffic backs up at one predictable intersection. People who don't want to wait or who are in a rush will nudge their way in from the left lane just before the traffic light. This is a defining moment in my mornings. If I decide to think compassionate thoughts, I smile, wave and let them in. But there will be no entering my lane when I choose malicious, judgmental thoughts. It is easy to lose focus of your Joy Factor in traffic, unless you're mindful.

You are the composer of your thoughts; no one drops by your home and deposits them into your subconscious mind. It may seem that others' words and actions affect us, yet when it comes right down to it, you decide what you're musing.

When you reverse the word responsibility, it reads "ability to respond." Your reaction to people and situations is based on your knack for being mindful and choosing the response that is optimal for *you*.

My friend Cathy prepared what she called her mother's "infamous" beef stew for dinner. As she was serving us this gorgeous bowl of goodness, she went on about its lack of flavor. "If I had my way, it would be spicier, but since this is the recipe my mom gave me, this is what I do." I reminded Cathy about her MSU and lo and behold, she adjusted her ingredients so her stew and her life had more zest.

People don't change for many reasons: fear, laziness, not knowing how. . . did I mention fear? As a lover of acronyms, I remember this one when change feels difficult.

Fantasized

Experience

Appearing

Real

Cathy was so uncertain of how her stew would turn out with a new spice that she let fear outweigh risk. What story are you making up that feels so real that it is stopping you from spicing things up?

I loved selling Aveda products to hair salons and spas for the thirteen years I was with Neill Corporation. When it was time to leave the safety of the corporate job and start my coaching business, I used my MSU every day. Here is a perfect example of how an MSU can be detrimental. I was paralyzed with fear for two years as I struggled with this decision. My fantasized experiences where like this:

What if no one hires me to coach them?

We will lose our home.

I will lose self-respect.

What will others think?

Matt won't love me anymore.

I will never be able to buy shoes again.

My fear-filled stories multiplied and grew. Finally, I paid attention to how I was using my MSU and shifted my thoughts accordingly. Nine years later, I have a successful coaching business, own two houses, celebrated my ten-year wedding anniversary in 2011, and have plenty of shoes (really cute ones, at that). The practice of this concept is where my power lies. You don't ever get to check fear off of your to-do list. But when you face it, the time between noticing your fear and making a shift to move past it gets shorter. When it shows up, it's the sign for you to begin to alter your story.

Every day you choose what "glasses" to wear, and they affect how you see the world. My story of change is not uncommon. A client was convinced she could not have a successful coaching business. A weeping willow was the image she held of herself as a business woman, which trapped her in her fearful story. We spent time reconnecting with what was most important to her—assessing her values and playing with various perspectives, until she chose to see herself as a glorious maple. The strong, new self-image helped drive her to create a successful business.

These experiences led me to create this acronym for love that came to me on my own journey of self-discovery.

Living
Our
Values
Every Day

When you Make Stuff Up that is more aligned with who you really are, you flow through life with new ease and joy. Values, which we'll speak more about in later chapters, are one of the elements in your process of making conscious decisions. An affirmation in my Louise Hay *I Can Do It* calendar was, "In any given situation you have a choice whether to focus on fear or love." What will you choose?

> *Sometimes your joy is the source of your smile, but sometimes your smile can be the source of your joy.*
>
> THICH NHAT HANH

"If you're happy and you know it clap your hands..." I loved to sing this old folk song as a kid with my first grade class. Jeanine was my best friend then and she loved it too. We would smile, laugh and see who could clap the loudest. It was so easy to express joy as a little kid. These days as a "joy strategist," joy and happiness have more impact than just clapping my hands. Happiness, well-being and contentment lead to manifesting desires. Is it coincidence on days I am feeling good and in the flow that I get front-row princess parking? When I leave a few minutes later than I need to and traffic parts like the Red Sea—is that happenstance? No, it is attraction in action, and it begins with a delightful mood and claiming my ability to attract from a place of joy.

There are many teachings and opinions about the Universal Laws of Attraction, which I will refer to as LOA. Some people state that all you have to do is think about your wishes and they will show up. Hocus pocus—like magic! Some days it is that easy. I believe there are more steps, though, to your dreams showing up without fail. My intention is not to teach you what the attraction principles are, but to show you that when you increase your Joy Factor, you will attract more of what you visualize. Feeling good is the start of having good things come to you, and these teachings will show you how.

When Rebecca Ewing is not beautifying a home or entertaining an audience, she is a master at finding how to feel good.

Friends and I were discussing how we comfort ourselves when we get stressed—or worse, depressed. "What are your comfort movies?" one asked. "What do you watch when it's been a hard day and you want to let it go?" **Secondhand Lions; Babette's Feast; Ever After.**

"Books?" asked another. Sue Bender's **Everyday Sacred** *always brings me back to center, or a riveting novel to take my mind somewhere else. Anything by Diana Gabaldon will transport me out of my doldrums.*

Knitting, sewing, or sometimes, cooking, can be a meditation when I'm too frazzled to meditate.

There is that snit, when I'm prickly, pissy and irritable, or that funky rut, where I can get stuck for too long if I don't have a plan. The right movie can break the state. Or an art gallery, a yarn store, or a field-trip to the design center. When I long for creative juice, Art—yes, the good stuff with a capital A—in most any form will awaken my mind and delight my senses.

From a deep or dark place, it takes more: I need to learn something, anything, that's new, interesting, engaging and fun. Courses in photography, drawing, painting, silversmithing, knitting and beading have each served as a path out of a long, heavy-laden winter of the spirit, in which I forgot that spring will come, always.

Recipe to Change My Life

Serves one; affects all

Preparation: *Take discontent and despair, place in that empty ice cream container, slap the lid on quickly, and put immediately in the trash.*

Ingredients: *1 question: What now?*

> *1 magazine, Google search, community newspaper or class listing*
>
> *1 spark of interest*
>
> *Research to taste*
>
> *1 decision*
>
> *1 registration*

Directions: *Gather supplies required for the course or workshop.*

Anticipate with eagerness.
Show up. Let go. Explore. Let loose. Stir often.
Repeat as needed.

When practicing the LOA, spending time figuring out *how* to achieve your intention can jam you up every time. Negative self-talk shows up and stops you in your tracks. Many clients I work with who are starting a business experience this type of "analysis paralysis." Karen became so stuck in trying to figure out the *hows* that it overwhelmed and squelched her passion. She walked away from her dream of opening a hair salon before she had truly tapped into her vision. She still laments her unfulfilled dream. This is a clear example of using her MSU in a detrimental manner. Knowing how to do certain things is important. For instance, changing a flat tire is a good thing to know. But having to know every specific detail about how something is going to come together can stand in the way of the magic of the principles of attraction. When you have to know and control everything, it does not contribute to the flow and ease available from allowing things to unfold.

When Rachelle gained clarity on the qualities she desired in a partner and let go of exactly how that person would look, her soul mate showed up. He looked different than the picture in her mind's eye. If she had remained attached to that image, she would have missed living life with her sweetheart.

Anyone can do anything that he imagines.

HENRY FORD

As a life-long learner, I have taken hundreds of courses over the years. TFAR was shared by T. Harv Eker, author of *Secrets of the Millionaire Mind*, at a Millionaire Mind Intensive I attended in Atlanta in 2007. This acronym will help you understand the power of your thinking.

Thoughts   Feelings   Actions   Results

Thoughts produce feelings. Feelings move you into action, or inaction. Actions produce results. If your thoughts leave you feeling good, you will experience the next stage of action, what I call inspired action. Inspired action leads to creating results with ease. The results you are looking for originate from your thoughts. It is a circular motion.

While driving home with my nephew Jake and sister Lisa, from his baseball practice, Jake wanted to listen to music; a typical request from a fifteen-year-old boy. Lisa and I were chatting while he picked his favorite station. The music he chose made my head hurt immediately and I could not believe the words that came out of my mouth: "What are you listening to?" I thought the music was horrid. He finally changed the station after a few moments of me begging to end the misery.

Thoughts are much like songs. When a song comes on the radio and you don't like it, simply change the station. If you don't change the station, then you end up being miserable. Why do you continue to listen to thoughts that do not lift you up? Or watch the local newscast? Or listen to people who grumble and gripe?

You don't have to monitor every thought; that would drive you insane. Noticing how you feel will give you the data you need about the power of your thoughts. Feeling good? Keep thinking what you are thinking. Not feeling so good? Shift your outlook.

The way you think today is a habit, and it can be changed. Think of other behaviors you have already altered. Most likely, the pain or

PHOTO BY PAT THOMAS

unhappiness in your life became so bad that you couldn't take it anymore. From knowing what you did *not* want, you were able to get clear on what you *did* want and began to create a new habit. It is the same when it comes to choosing joy. When you move forward toward your desires with inspired action, the Universe will lean in to meet you. This part of the LOA principles are the fundamental piece that many people miss. Giant steps are not necessary, for small movements based on inspired action are monumental. If you are not feeling good, your next action step is to do what is going to make you feel better. Period.

At spin class, Kim, our mistress of torture, (I mean fitness instructor) consistently reminds us to make minute adjustments in both our body and attitude to enjoy the class and receive the most benefit. Little shifts make a big difference.

What are the small modifications in your life that will make your to-do list feel more like inspired action? Perhaps listening to music, reading something inspirational, or dancing. If connecting with nature is for you, then enjoy the following recipe from Vanessa Lowry—girlfriend, marketing consultant, graphic designer, speaker, author and all around joy enthusiast.

Nature's Recipe for Joy

I learned at an early age that my fun times often were outside. As I've gotten older, I've found that walking outdoors, paddling my kayak and riding my bike soothes life's prickly edges. I come back inside with new ideas and enthusiasm for moving forward. My sense of gratitude expands as I see the abundance in nature.

Nature's recipe engages all your senses. You may vary the ratio of ingredients according to your preference and the result is never the same. For me, nature always opens the door to Joy.

SIGHT:

Look for contrasts. Marvel in the sweeping views from a mountain overlook, then focus in on the stamens of a flower or the colors of a caterpillar. Look down and notice how the sunlight paints shadows on the ground. Look up and name the shapes of clouds in the sky.

SOUND:

Take off your earbuds and stop conversation for a few minutes. Hear the breeze rustling the grass or a choir of crickets. Listen closer and you might hear a squirrel chattering or an eagle call. The more you practice listening, the more you hear.

SMELL:

I find that places and seasons have a particular smell and can pull up wonderful memories. Stop and take a deep breath. Do you smell a hint of summer jasmine? The tang of fall leaves? What do you appreciate about the person or the particular time of your life that comes to mind?

TOUCH:

Let your body's largest organ, your skin, get into the act. Notice the breeze touching your ears and face. Skim leaf edges with your fingertip as you pass by.

TASTE:

Smell and taste are closely related. The scent of a ripe tomato just off the vine makes the taste even more delicious.

This recipe is great when life gets particularly busy with work and other tasks. Start today and commit to include Nature's Recipe for Joy into your diet more often.

When I got involved with the SimpleWealth coaching program, my intention was to become a millionaire real estate investor. That was in 2008 when the bottom dropped out of the market. I forged ahead with a good dose of trust and supportive people at my side, toward my goal of prosperity and success. Instead of becoming a real estate mogul, the Joy Factor blog site was born. From there, I took a few steps forward and a few more backwards—it was an interesting dance. This book is the manifestation of my original intention. It looks nothing like my initial goal, yet it is bringing me more joy and satisfaction than I could have imagined. When manifestation happens from a place of allowing, it feels magical and so right that you may look back and think, "How did that happen?" This is the beauty of

TFAR. When your thoughts and feelings are aligned, your actions and results will be the evidence of that alignment.

As I was growing up and finding my way in life, my mom frequently asked, "If everyone else jumped off a bridge, would you?" Of course—I yearned to belong, so I would have surely taken the leap. Ironically, hurdling to my potential death to follow everyone else was about as far from Authentic Expression and mindful decisions as one could get. If I only knew then what I do now: fitting in does not contribute to sustainable happiness. As a conscious creator, you pick thoughts, feelings and actions that align with your Joy Factor. You pay attention to what is happening in the moment and make choices that serve you and others.

Conscious creation is another foundational philosophy in this life-enhancing process. Adopting this perspective will move you from operating on automatic pilot to being the thoughtful caretaker of your reality.

Mary's relationship ended after nine years. As she uncovered what was really important to her and she started putting her attention on these things, her daily decisions reflected her true desires. Slowly but surely, her life was filled with more of what she had been craving—a connection to spirit, friends and family, creativity and time with her dog. This was life-changing for her, and a joy to witness.

How many people do you know who have everything you think would bring happiness? For example, they have a seemingly good relationship, nice house, nice car, good job and yet, they are still not happy, and may even be downright miserable. Even though it seems like external things bring happiness, the happiness is not long-lasting.

Sustainable joy and happiness begin with conscious choice. Do the things that make you happy now. Start small. Something that raises my Joy Factor is to sing. I cannot carry a tune, yet singing always lifts my spirit. From there, I can take the next step toward the direction I want to go and *voilá*, modest but mighty manifestations happen.

Award-winning chefs use the best ingredients and tools to make dishes to earn the coveted Michelin star rating. As a conscious creator using the Law of Attraction, your MSU, TFAR and the Joy Factor ingredients, your life will get a three-star rating. Choose the ingredients that are tasty to you, partner that with the right utensils, and you are on your way to creating a marvelous life.

Cookery is not chemistry. It is an art. It requires instinct and taste rather than exact measurements.

MARCEL BOULESTIN

ART BY KAY WISCHKAEMPER

Chapter 4

Follow Your
Passionate
Breadcrumbs

LEE GOSS PHOTOGRAPHY

Chapter 4

Follow Your Passionate Breadcrumbs

If passions are the breadcrumbs that lead to a fulfilling life, where do you find these tasty morsels? I'm not talking about the ones in a flip-top can on aisle three of your favorite grocery store. You'll find these passion breadcrumbs only when you slow down and ponder what living your best life looks like. The answer is found where passion—the kind that brings you fully alive, resides: in your heart.

I attended a party with my husband and thought to ask the other guests what brought them delight. It was no surprise that nearly everyone found their greatest pleasure in their work or family, but many did not know what they really relished. They appeared to answer from their head without consulting their heart, and their responses held little energy.

This chapter explores the mysterious focal point where passion resides. Opening to possibilities of this powerful head-to-heart connection can be better than the finest chocolate that has ever melted on your tongue: nearly rapturous. Passion is that intense interest or enthusiasm that brings the *most* joy and aliveness.

In May of 2010, Eli Moises Velcro Watkins became a member of our family. An eighteen-month-old wolfhound mix was a perfect match for Abbey Road, our nine-year-old Australian shepherd. Intense enthusiasm seems to be their religion, their way of life. Whether eating, playing, sleeping or stalking the squirrels, they do everything full-out. When they want love, they ask for it. When they want to give love, they do—sometimes by licking my face in the middle of the night. Their lives are focused on one thing: what brings them the most joy.

If they were able to contribute a recipe, this is what it would be:

A Perfectly Passionate Doggy Day
by Abbey and Eli

1. Begin each day with a huge stretch and yawn.

2. Wag your tail.

3. Get someone to pet you and love on you.

4. Give kisses.

5. Go outside and romp in the fresh air.

6. Eat something delicious.

7. Wag your tail.

8. Chase a squirrel.

9. Play with the ball or favorite toy.

10. Take a nap.

> *11. Eat some cookies.*
>
> *12. Repeat steps 1-11 for the rest of the day and night.*

I have learned a tremendous amount about passion from Abbey and Eli, particularly, their rapt attention to what they love. Their focus is on getting what they want. And they do, especially cookies.

PHOTO BY WENDY WATKINS

In 1995, at thirty-three years old, I was bitten by the marriage bug; it was time for me to get serious about finding my perfect partner. Every Monday night, I met with my friend Kris, and we worked our way, one chapter per week, through Sonia Choquette's book, *Creating Your Heart's Desire*, then we shared dinner and watched *Ali McBeal*. These nights were satisfying for the next three months, even though the man of my dreams did not knock on my door and ask me to marry him. Yet I was open, curious and (somewhat) patient.

The following summer, my sister's best friend invited several people to join him in Hawaii. Whoever could get themselves there would have a free place to stay. I had known him for ten years, and as we spent more time together planning our trip, I began to feel amorous towards him. It was strange, but I went with it. One thing led to another, and in 2001, Matt and I went back to Hawaii to be wed.

Passion can be expressed as a feeling of unusual excitement, enthusiasm or compelling emotion towards a subject, idea, person, or object. When you have passion for something, you have a strong affinity for it, and when you put your attention on it, magic happens. I wanted a luscious, committed relationship with a man I admire, respect and enjoy. I knew he would love my family, my friends, and my animals. He would be smart and funny. He would be romantic, adorable, and healthy. I imagined him every day.

And then, one day, there he was.

Before I knew what was most important to me, I was the Queen of Numb; food, cigarettes, prescription drugs, a little of this, a few more pairs of shoes—a quick substitute for joy—and then I was back for more abuse of my body, mind and spirit. I floundered for years.

Evidence of disconnected, dispassionate indifference in our culture is visible at nearly every turn. Obesity, depression, consumer debt and substance abuse: alcohol, and drugs, whether prescription, recreational or illegal, are all the results of a society laden by despair. We don't need another study, infomercial, YouTube clip or Facebook status to know that too many people lack life-affirming passion.

What is it that keeps folks in a rut, wearing blinders? I have a multi-part response to this question.

1) Most people do not know how to uncover what they love most, and

2) They don't realize living a passion-filled life is an option.

It is time for **you** to get out of the bread line and use new utensils and wholesome ingredients to get some delicious new results.

The movie *Precious* was about a young woman living in the ghetto with a horribly abusive mother, who would never have known there was a different way to live had her school principal not recognized her potential. Once Precious glimpsed what was possible, she became a conscious creator. Whether she knew it or not, she got her MSU and things started turning around for her. She began with clear, wholehearted desire, and took baby steps. Education is important, but not more so than what drives our lives. Living without passion is an option, until it isn't. Precious uncovered the zest for her life journey.

There are multiple ways to discover personal purpose: books, discussions, therapy, workshops and tests top the list. One of the best tools is the *New York Times* bestseller, *The Passion Test*, by Chris Attwood and Janet Bray Attwood. The process they provide to uncover your passions is simple and profound, and made a huge impact on my life. The resonance of truth rocked my world when I realized that my purpose is to be a healer, helping people to fully bloom. Through PassionFruit, my coaching business, I am a "creative people grower."

When something tastes that delicious, I have to share it. In 2009, I became a certified facilitator of *The Passion Test*. Since then, I've used it with hundreds of clients and the results are consistently and predictably miraculous.

It is a test you can never fail. You identify your top five passions, align your life around them and watch a world of possibilities open up.

When Mike came for coaching, he had an enchanting relationship with his wife and experienced joy and abundance in many other areas, but . . . after taking *The Passion Test*, he knew two things: he had to change his career and pay attention to his health.

Clarity is powerful. Mike called the very next day to report that he was laid off from his job. He stated calmly that he was relieved, joyful and optimistic about his future, and as he released his old work paradigm, there was room to create the new.

Today, Mike enjoys a business partnership with an accomplished designer who creates and produces unique lighting and tables. This fits with his passion of "working with architecture and design," and allows him "free time to enjoy a fun life" (another passion) and to explore his enthusiasm for food and wine. Health wise, Mike is holding at ten pounds lighter and staying very active.

When asked how he stays focused on his passions, Mike says, "We always get off track from time to time and one way I get back on focus is to review the Passion Card Wendy encouraged me to make. Along with my passions on the front of the card, I also included some helpful tidbits on the back. Remembering to 'get out of my own way' and that 'life is created out of the things to which I give attention' allows me to 'choose in favor of my passions' when I face a decision. No one is perfect and certainly not me, so I learned that getting off track occasionally is a normal occurrence but getting back on track and refocusing on my passions is when I would feel the best about what I am doing and how I am living."

ART BY VANESSA LOWRY

Our society moves at breakneck speeds, as do I: my alter ego is known as Wendy Andretti. I'll be zooming down the highway and Matt will ask, "Did you just see those beautiful flowers?" I respond, "No! Where?" And he says the ones we just blew past. If I were to slow down, I would be able to see so much more of what I adore.

*Passion surprises.
One doesn't search
it. It can happen
to you tomorrow.*

ISABELLE ADJANI

Start in your heart. Listen there and the beat will give you an extraordinary, fresh song that includes whispers and inklings of ideas to titillate and excite. The inner critic wags a finger in your face and challenges you to figure everything out, submit a plan, and follow it exactly. That critic is trying to control when the need is to let the dream unfold. That pesky inner voice will raise your blood pressure, not your Joy Factor.

From your heart, you calibrate your thoughts and beliefs to manifest your passions and purpose. The two-foot drop from the head to the heart is a sweet journey if your heart is there to catch you. Otherwise, you ricochet back to your head. It can be a bummer of a bungee jump.

In the movie, *Julie and Julia*, both women had a passion for cooking. Each demonstrated it in different ways. They may have had doubts, yet I believe they stayed connected to their heart and head. No matter how much Julia Childs loved food, had she used only logic, would we have had all of those delicious recipes? Probably not.

Most people waver back and forth between head and heart: it is a predictable, and valuable experience. In the heart lives faith and trust. Combine that with clarity and focus and your Joy Factor will blossom.

"It is what it is" is a statement of either acceptance or resignation. This speaks to my second response to a consistent disconnection from passion which is not realizing that living a passion-filled life is an option. Just because you have always done it a certain way, or your mother has done it that way, or your co-workers do it that way, does not mean you have to do it that way.

Sugar is a like drug to me, and once I have a little, I want more. When I am on a sweet kick, it is hard to get a good workout at the

PHOTO BY PAT THOMAS

gym. I feel like a car that has been filled with crappy gasoline: I stop, start, and maybe, stall. In my mind, I chant, "No more cookies. No more cookies."

When I remember that I want a fulfilling life, I recall that to feel different I have to do something different. I put away the chocolate chip cookie recipe and use this one instead.

Doing it Differently

1 part intense desire for something else

1 part boredom of what currently is

1 small part clarity of what I desire

1 part willingness to focus on that desire

1 part optimism

Sift through the part that is boring. Remove the big chunks of dullness and compost immediately. Pour in your intense desire. Add clarity and focus. Sprinkle in just enough optimism and place into your heart.

Serve it every time you desire something new. Bonus—enjoy it with a whole different group of people and notice the enhanced flavor.

With just a touch of college under my belt, the idea of writing a book felt more like a dream than reality. My inner critic would persuade me that I was not smart enough. However, after running a successful coaching business for more than eight years, I knew I had more to contribute. Uncompromising self-examination gave me the idea and the commitment to write *The Joy Factor Recipe Book*. First, I had successfully given up the self-abuse of using drugs. Second, I saw that I was "walking my talk." I had, and continue to, embrace the personal development concepts that I know work. As I integrated the utensils and ingredients I speak of here, with my crystal-clear vision of a world of joyful conscious creators, I knew in my heart of hearts it was time to write this book. Once the lid was taken off this jar of passion, there was no stopping me.

Don't get me wrong, there were times that I was filled with doubt, like when the goal felt unreachable. Then my heart would fill with desire, moving me forward with ease and, of course, joy. I found the right people to help with the parts I don't do well, and I did what I was good at: sharing my vision, wisdom and experience. The rest fell into place.

I was excited by the revelation that in writing a book I was honoring my passion. I turned down the volume on the negative thoughts, and rode the emotional roller coaster that comes with such a big-gulp project. As I gave myself permission to experience the highs and lows, the doubts and the certainty, I moved forward slowly, in fits and starts. Did I mention slowly? And here you are, holding the manifestation of my healing, my desire, actions, commitment and purpose.

> *There is no passion to be found playing small—in settling for a life that is less than the one you are capable of living.*
>
> NELSON MANDELA

Knowing *how* you are going to live a passion-filled life can throw you for a loop. When I am driving somewhere that I have never been before, I can become obsessed about having clear, precise directions. Matt does the opposite, he is okay with having an idea of where we are going, trusting we'll eventually arrive at our destination. I believe that life is about the journey, not the destination, so why are directions so darn important to me? Perhaps I am such a visionary that, without direction, I lose focus and travel round and round without making headway. Would it be so bad if I made a few wrong turns along the way?

When I go in a different direction than I anticipated, and I decide that it is an adventure, then the journey is enjoyable and I'm open to possibilities. If I deem that turn to be wrong and I beat myself up about it, the first step to a less-than-joyful perspective has taken hold, and it is a downward spiral from there.

Enjoying the journey requires us to notice our perspectives. One of my life lessons is to slow down. When I am moving too fast, I tend to make unconscious decisions, and wonder where the joy has gone.

How long have you been sleeping on the same side of the bed? Six weeks? Six months? Six years? Every six to eight months, Matt and I change it up. It is a simple practice to keep our change-muscle limber.

Fear of change is the third reason most people miss enjoying a passion-filled journey. Some will use their MSU to keep them right where they are, stuck in their dread, wedged in the territory of uncomfortably comfortable, a.k.a familiar. Most people are convinced that evolution is always tough, and would rather walk around in old, beat-up shoes than wear new ones that are comfortable and supportive.

How many people do you know who do not like, much less love, their job, yet stay? Think of the relationships we endure, cities where we live, the clothes and hairstyles we wear year after year.

I propose a novel perspective: change is good. François de La Rochefoucauld, a French classical author in the late 1600s said, "The only thing constant in life is change." Change may not be painless, yet as you experience it more, just like wearing those new shoes, it becomes comfortable. Rochefoucauld also said that "When we are unable to find tranquility within ourselves, it is useless to seek it elsewhere." Passion gives you the peace and verve for which you yearn.

I am not talking change for sake of change. Not everything has to be altered to create a good recipe. I am suggesting that a rearrangement can make your life rich and delicious, like your favorite piece of pie. You know what recipes are not working for you. Since you are doing it differently now, why not try a piece of Change Pie?

Change Pie

1 part trust

1 part desire

1 part clarity

1 part ask for help

Mix the ingredients together to preserve their essence.
When you are ready to move forward, add the following:

1 part confidence

1 part inspired action

Pour into a pie pan greased with love. Bake until you are done doing it the way you have been and are ready to do things differently. Top with your favorite affirmation and serve with a cup of vitality.

My experience is that our passions will eventually change and evolve. That doesn't mean they are no longer a primary pleasure, just that they're naturally present in your life. Now there is time and space for a new passion to emerge.

Allow me to share a distinction between passion and purpose. Purpose is the essence of who you are, the title of the recipe of your life. It is the big picture of what you have come here to do. I am here to be a successful healer, someone who can communicate with people to help them help themselves. My passions are the ingredients in this recipe to fulfill my purpose. The difference between purpose and passion is a fine line. Think of it this way:

WENDY'S RECIPE

Successful Healer—Purpose

Which includes the passion of being a:

- People Grower
- Joy Strategist
- Writer
- Speaker

- Passion Test Facilitator
- Strategic Attractionist

All of these fall under the umbrella of honoring my purpose, of who I be.

Be, Do, Have is a model that my godfather, Dr. Larry Markson, success and personal growth coach to thousands and author of *Talking to Yourself is Not Crazy*, shared with me.

A Recipe for Being, Doing and Having

Being happy, healthy, fulfilled, successful and in love are all inside-out experiences! You will not, and cannot, be happy and satisfied with your life if your happiness and satisfaction are determined by the things that happen to you.

The work ethic that we have been programmed to believe states that when you HAVE the things you want, you will DO the things you need to do, and then you will BE happy. But, life doesn't really work that way!

It is imperative for you to understand and know that the Doing and Having parts of your life are not what make life work. The Being part, on the other hand, is the secret ingredient that makes life work by energetically attracting all the people, places, things and circumstances into your life to make it a masterpiece.

It is the actual flow of life—Be, Do and Have (20% of the population—the winners in life) vs. Have, Do and Be (80% of the population—those who struggle and are always trying to survive and just get by).

If you are BEING happy and satisfied, you will automatically be DOING what happy and satisfied people are doing, and you will HAVE the things you want to have.

BE, DO and HAVE is the fundamental principle of success, and it states that, "Your life and how you feel and what you get are determined by YOU!" Scary, huh? You create your own success or you are the cause of your own failures. It is never from the outside, always from the inside-out.

Success comes FROM you, not TO you!!

Success in any undertaking is about clarity, about BEING on purpose, about BEING centered and BEING in touch with the higher power within. Furthermore, success in all its ramifications is about BEING congruent and in total alignment between "who you are" and "what you do."

You can only HAVE complete success, happiness and satisfaction in your life when your mission is accomplished (whatever that may be), when your talents are developed (the expert utilization of who you are inside your skin) and your destiny is fulfilled (to be one with the Universe and to walk hand in hand with someone you unconditionally love.)

Then, and only then, will you finally BE and reach the art of inner peace, serenity and complete fulfillment.

If you do not inherently know your purpose, this chapter will be valuable. As the conscious creator of your delicious life, you weren't meant to go through this creation process alone. Find the person, tool, book, or experience to support you in finding your resolution in life.

In the meantime, consider these questions:

- If you knew you only had five years to live, what legacy would you want to leave?
- Why is this legacy important?
- What is important about this reason?

Continue asking yourself what is important. Your answers may look something like mine:

My intended legacy is for people to know that they can do whatever it is they want in life while enjoying their journey. It is important to me because too many people are struggling and don't know any other way. It is important to share resources so people have access to a different way of doing things. That is important because if I did not learn alternate ways of living my life, I would not be where I am today. This is important because my experience can help others. My purpose is to help others.

A clear path will open once you detect an inkling of your purpose and blend it with your passions. The key is to be open to unmasking and claiming it. It shows up as a feeling, craving or deep desire to pursue or create something more. What you are experiencing is the essence of your purpose. Don't push it aside like an over-cooked side dish. Don't tolerate a so-so life because it is easier than changing.

> *Passion is energy. Feel the power that comes from focusing on what excites you.*
>
> OPRAH WINFREY

As a young girl, I had an idea that I wanted to help others, evidenced in my choices of friends and boyfriends. My parents called me the "defender of the underdog." Having the ability to see possibilities for others before they could see them for themselves led me to hang out with people who had a lack of vision and direction.

I put attention on what was important to me, which was personal development and having a good time. I found job after job where I could use my passions and leadership skills. I was thirty-seven years old when I discovered life coaching—it came up on the screen as I searched the Web for ways to become a better mentor in my job. This was to be the next evolution of my purpose and passion.

Roberta Coker was a professional chef and worked in the restaurant business for more than twenty years before she became a hand analyst. We met in 2003, when I was leaving my corporate job and growing into my own purpose, the one she helped me define by reading the lines in my hands. Enjoy Roberta's recipe:

Being on Purpose

I was not a baker (baking is a science, cooking is an art), so to me a recipe is merely an idea or an outline meant to be messed with, changed according to personal taste, and approached with a sense of adventure. My method for creating a masterpiece is to list all the possible appropriate ingredients and then use my experience, intuition, and taste buds to tell me how to put it together, how much of each ingredient to use, and when it's ready to serve.

The Recipe For Being On Purpose

(according to Roberta...)

Ingredients (in order of importance):

Desire/Yearning—*what is burning inside you, regardless of seeming time constraints, others' judgments, or perceived lack of capital?*

Permission—*it's okay to be BIG; as a matter of fact, it's necessary, as Marianne Williamson shares from **A Return to Love: Reflections on the Principles of "A Course in Miracles"**-*

Our deepest fear is not that we are inadequate.

*Our deepest fear is that we are
powerful beyond measure.*

*It is our light, not our darkness,
that most frightens us.
We ask ourselves
"Who am I to be brilliant, gorgeous,
talented and fabulous?"*

*Actually, who are you NOT to be?
You are a child of God.*

*Your playing small doesn't serve the world.
There's nothing enlightened about shrinking so that
other people won't feel insecure around you.*

*We were born to make manifest the glory of God within us.
It's not just in some of us; it's in EVERYONE!*

*And as we let our own light shine, we unconsciously
give other people permission to do the same.*

*As we are liberated from our own fear,
our presence automatically liberates others!*

Service to others/Depth of vision—*when you look at an acorn, do you see a meal for a squirrel, a single tree, a forest, or a housing development made from the wood of the forest's trees?*

Truth/Authenticity/Integrity/Compassion—*the first person to whom you have to tell the truth is you, and that can be a very humbling experience…your thoughts, your words, and your actions need to be in alignment. And whether you are a physician or not, you should adhere to the part of the Hippocratic Oath that speaks of doing no harm.*

Presence/Centeredness/Grounded/Knowing and upholding your own Boundaries—*breathe deeply, regularly.*

Clarity/Definition/Focus/Priorities—*it is important to be clear about what is important to you.*

Joy/Fun/Passion/Emotion/Intuition—*without these, you're basically dead.*

Commitment/Obsession/Faith/Belief/Willingness to change—*without these, there will be no forward movement.*

Positive Attitude/Gratitude—*without these, you will experience only sorrow.*

Risk-taking/Action/Perseverance—*absolutely necessary ingredients, at some point, in order to experience fulfillment and success, the more often added, the better.*

Excitement/Anticipation—*let the feeling build until you think you might actually explode.*

Sprinkle generously throughout entire process:
> *Self-respect*
>
> *Self-worth*
>
> *Self-acceptance*
>
> *Self-promotion*

*Under **NO** circumstances add:*
> *Conformity/Obligation/Self-sacrifice*
> *(especially important to stay away from*
> *in the Desire/Yearning, Permission, and the*
> *Service to others/Depth of vision phases)*
>
> *Worry*
>
> *Doubt*
>
> *Harsh Self-critique*
>
> *Harsh Self-judgment*

Remember to experiment. You can't be afraid to make mistakes—they were invented to build confidence, you know.

"Whether you think you can or you think you can't, you're right!" ~ Henry Ford

Patience, another quality of living a joy-filled life, plays a key role in honing our purpose and passions. Grasping the concepts of being a conscious creator is, theoretically, straightforward. We read the books, attend the talks and learn the method; that is the easy part. Putting these theories into practice, well, it takes practice. As you consistently integrate this knowledge, it becomes a way of life, not just a theory, and as much as we wish otherwise, it doesn't happen overnight.

I have made Leroy Bars, a delicious dessert, hundreds of times, and I no longer need to read the recipe. Likewise, I have been practicing affirmations for twenty years. Both of these things help me enjoy my life. The affirmations keep my attention on what it is I desire and well, Leroy Bars are delicious and so fun to share. Having only practiced meditation for a year, I still need direction. Do I beat myself up that I don't know how to meditate yet? No, I'm still learning. It takes practice, and then more practice, and patience. Affirm with me, "I am patient."

Over the years, the quality of my relationships has evolved. When I was younger, I enjoyed a lot of friends. Fifty-plus people often attended the soirees we hosted for any given occasion. I've grown selective about who I spend my time with. I prefer a gathering of six to eight people. I favor being able to relate individually. It's not about quantity, but quality. I want to be with people who are positive, honest and purposeful; those who are joyful and conscious.

As your Joy Factor blooms, you, too, will be different, and the people closest to you will want you to stay the same. They liked the person they could complain to, criticize and gossip with. It may be uncomfortable at first, but some relationships may fall away. The gift is that as you release the old; you open up space for a new, like-minded community.

Mahatma Ghandi said, *"Be the change you wish to see in the world."*

Wendy Watkins says, *"Increase your Joy Factor to live the life you love."*

Martin Luther King, Jr. was a clergyman, activist, and prominent leader in the African-American Civil Rights movement. His passions were apparent in everything he did, from giving amazing speeches and leading non-violent demonstrations, to laying the groundwork for the repeal of racial segregation and discrimination laws. He received the Noble Peace Prize for his actions. I believe that his core passion was to love and serve humanity, and his purpose was to lead the movement—a perfect blend which made his influence great. Did everyone love Dr. King? Absolutely not. Did that stop him?

Honoring your passions takes many shapes. Yours may not be as grand as King's, yet it is imperative to make sure they come from your heart. This is your distinct journey, and your enthusiasm will direct you in your march.

I fell in love with cycling when I started riding with friends in 2008. One day, I heard myself say, "I'm going to ride a century." Caught up in the moment, I thought this personal challenge would be easy. After two years of training, I was ready to tackle the task of riding one hundred miles on my bicycle in a day.

It was a glorious morning and my entire being was ready to go. My physical training had my body ready for the task. Now, it was up to my mind and spirit. While the end goal of 100 miles was daunting, I knew there were rest stops every fifteen miles, so I told myself that all I needed to do was ride fifteen miles, then fifteen more, and so on. Seven times I repeated that mantra, and my goal was accomplished. My body kept up with my mind and spirit, as my mind and spirit urged my body. I crossed the finish line with tears in my eyes, and celebrated

PHOTO BY PAT THOMAS

meeting this personal challenge. I relish the experience, from the idea, to the training, to the ride to the finish. It was an amazing day.

Over and over, I've seen people who take on more than they can chew, then become overwhelmed and do nothing. That's *not* a good recipe. Clarify your purpose first. Next, create your plan. A Joyful Passion Plan is the perfect way to approach a big-gulp goal and spread it out into doable pieces.

Joyful Passion Plan

1. *Clarify your passions.*
2. *Uncover and align with your purpose.*
3. *Imagine the proof of living a joyfully passionate life.*
4. *Think about yourself enjoying this excitement for a few minutes each day.*
5. *Deeply experience the feeling that comes with visualizing you living your passion.*
6. *Take baby steps forward each day.*
7. *Celebrate your accomplishments daily.*
8. *Create a visual reminder of your passion and purpose.*
9. *Create an audio reminder of your passion and purpose.*
10. *Create a support team, i.e. a mastermind group, professional coach, personal assistant, etc.*
11. *Allow for magic and miracles to show up in your life—notice and celebrate them when they do.*

On paper, the Joyful Passion Plan has a lot of moving parts. While some of them seem easier than others, the key, regardless how big or small, is to begin working your plan. Now.

People who are pleased with their Joy Factor make choices that align with their passions to make them successful. Imagine what that would be for you, and take a few minutes to write your plan.

YOUR JOYFUL PASSION PLAN

My Passion is: _____

_____

_____

_____

Each day I will:

1. _____

2. _____

3. _____

4. _____

5. _____

My reminders of my passions are:

1. _____

2. _____

3. _____

The intended result of aligning with this passion is: _____

_____

_____

_____

_____

_____

_____

When you live in alignment with your passion and purpose, you are happier, which means you are more connected to yourself, which allows you to connect with other people from a place of love and kindness. A positive ripple effect spreads to the next person, and the next. Soon, you are dreaming, and living your dream. Some people think this is selfish or indulgent, in light of world hunger, war, and appalling poverty. I request that you reframe that thought. How can you not?

When Johnny Appleseed decided to provide people with food, he started his trees by planting apple seeds. Yes, those little brown seeds that are in every apple. He traveled, sharing these seeds and seedlings so that others could have apple trees.

I watched a show on PBS about the Blue Man Group. The interviewer asked about their early days: "What did people think of you showing up in bars, in blue body paint, banging on whatever you were banging on?" People thought they were crazy, but they knew that this is what they loved. They said that they were, "following their bliss path." They used their MSU and the first ingredient of the Joy Factor. These days, they sell out arenas around the world, and appear to be living lives they truly love.

Passion rebuilds the world for the youth. It makes all things alive and significant.

RALPH WALDO EMERSON

Living your passions is not too hard for others, but worrying what they will think can make it hard for you to swallow. Use your MSU in a way that supports you. Make Stuff Up that says, "my friends and family want me to live a life that I am madly in love with." When you think those thoughts, your feelings change. Notice the difference in thinking that they want you to truly enjoy your life versus they do not want you to live a life you love. The thought shifts your vibration. The idea creates a feeling that moves you into action. A thought is just a thought—something that you choose to think.

Most people look at what is, complain about it, get more of it, complain more, and blame others. Living a fulfilling life is a radical act. Taking responsibility for your life is a different story. Have you ever been in a traffic jam, say, stopped on a major interstate? To your left is someone in their vehicle, about to explode, rigid white knuckles gripping the steering wheel. From the car on the right comes music, and the driver is singing out loud and seat-dancing, bouncing to the beat. They're both stuck in traffic. The distinction is how they respond. To one, it is a messy, bothersome situation. The other rejoices in the moment.

How do you respond to the state of affairs in your life? Are you grooving to the music or are you white-knuckled and ticked off? You get to decide. My friend Deb keeps a jar of liquid bubbles in her glove box for just such an occasion. Drivers near her idled car usually gaze in wonder as she begins blessing them with small, iridescent orbs floating in the air.

Your Joy Factor grows when you find the perfect ingredients to weave into your daily recipe. Passion and purpose will add zest and zeal. Choose passion. Choose purpose. Choose a delicious life.

> *"Nothing great in the world has ever*
> *been accomplished without passion."*
> - GEORG WILHELM FRIEDRICH HEGEL

What is Your Recipe for Passion? _____

_____

_____

_____

_____

_____

_____

_____

_____

_____

_____

_____

_____

_____

_____

_____

_____

_____

_____

_____

*Authentic
expression
always wins.*

WENDY WATKINS

Chapter 5

Your
Unique
Flavor

*Self-love and
acceptance
is the basis for
sustainable change.*

WENDY WATKINS

Chapter 5

Your Unique Flavor

The slogan, "It's the real thing," referred to the original recipe of Coca-Cola. The success of this beverage was phenomenal, unlike New Coke that was introduced in 1985. This bubbly thirst quencher was positioned as "the new taste of Coca-Cola." The general public, especially the Southeast, home of Coke, rebelled. They demanded their coke back and after a boycott, the original formula was reintroduced only three months later.

Are you aligned with the real you?

I first saw Chely Wright while watching *The Ellen DeGeneres Show*. Chely was the first major country artist to come out as gay. Yes, K.D. Lang came out in 1992, but she had abandoned the country music genre by then. It took courage for Chely to express herself authentically, and she opened the door for others to do the same. There's a lot of external pressure to be like everyone else, or what others expect, and being honest can make one achingly vulnerable.

Authenticity means being genuine and original, as opposed to being a fake or reproduction. Expression is a way of communicating something, or how you present yourself in the world. When it feels real, you are expressing yourself authentically.

In a blog post on The Joy Factor website, writer and color goddess, Rebecca Ewing, tells about an older woman she met in a nursing home. Unlike the other residents, she was dressed, complete with stockings and sensible shoes, hair styled and sprayed, and wearing lipstick. "Bright red-orange lipstick. ALL over her mouth. And cheeks. Lipstick by Picasso!"

Rebecca's first impulse was to offer to help the woman put the makeup on "right." Then she realized it was a criticism in disguise, driven by her head sense of being proper. When Rebecca listened to her heart, she knew that the woman's toothy smile that went—literally—from ear to ear, was perfect.

"If I'm ever in Mrs. Whitton's seat, wearing too much beige and a hairstyle thirty years out-of-date, with rare neuro-connections, I pray I remember the joy of a good lipstick," says Rebecca.

This story is ripe with Joy Factor ingredients. One is giving more credence to the heart than the head. The other is the dear crone's authenticity, knowing, from years of experience, that pretty lipstick makes her look and, most important, feel better.

People pick up on genuine communication; there is an unmistakable resonance to truth. But the most important point here is that you feel connected to yourself. One way that we do that is through our self-talk. This internal voice becomes the author of our stories, our recipes and cookbook. It may sound something like this:

How does my hair look?

Did I leave the iron on?

Will my boss like my presentation?

What's for lunch?

Does she like me? Respect me?

This mental chatter can range from mundane to exotic. We know these thoughts produce feelings and actions. Positive self-talk supports you in building a solid foundation of self-esteem. You are making up the questions, so compose answers that you want to hear.

Along those lines, Fran Asaro, Life Coach extraordinaire, suggests that we:

Make It Up As We Go Along

How in the world do we get all the wisdom that we have by the time we are up in years? Where did we get the data, the rules, the wherewithal, to become the person we are becoming?

Some follow other's advice. We do what we are told and trust that it will provide the way. Then there are those of us who make it all up as we go along. You get to decide what type of human being you want to be; what type of parent; what type of boss or employee you wish to become. Sometimes you don't realize it but you are the one who gets to choose throughout your entire life, the quality of it, and the joy that you experience. Yes, you are that powerful.

During challenging times I wonder, "how did I get myself in this circumstance?" and then I realize that nothing happens without my participation. So I choose again. I make up a new path, a new routine, and yes, even a new way of being, so that my life continues to unfold into my ideal.

One time I decided I was worth more than I was earning. I made up a new acceptable income for myself. Within a year I reached it. I also made up my own attitude about every day occurrences. I made up the notion that it all turns into gold anyway so why not be in the best spirit I can while I am faced with hurdles.

Life is a game. This alone makes it fun, but when it becomes YOUR game and you know how to make it all up as you go along, imagine how alive it feels.

Affirmation for today: "I am the designer of my life. I create it from this day forward."

Louise Hay's bestselling book, *You Can Heal Your Life*, is where I learned about positive affirmations. Years of inner chatter didn't serve me well:

You are not good enough.

Nobody loves you.

You are a fraud.

Learning to embrace the subtle yet powerful process of affirmations was how I began to change my story. I discovered how to conceive from a place of healthy, authentic expression, and at first, my recipe was palatable, then outright delicious.

The gift that I open again and again from Louise is the confidence, power and wisdom of self-love and acceptance. This *is* the basis for sustainable change. It's imperative to adore yourself just as you are, and at the same time, focus on the kind of person you want to become. That is the essence of enjoying the journey. Where you are right now is perfect. Embrace who you are and allow the next step to unfold.

I met Louise at the 2011 *I Can Do It Conference* in Tampa, Florida. This woman speaks from an authentic core of balance and certainty, and the love and power behind her words is tangible. I've been studying her teachings since the early eighties and I hold her in the highest esteem. My longing to meet her in person, and to tell her the impact she has made in my life, was keen.

On Saturday, I went to meet her and have my book signed. As I walked up to the line I was told Louise was done for the day, and to come back tomorrow. The next day after lunch, I sauntered to the book-signing area with a coffee and book to read if the line was long. I turned the corner, and to my pleasant surprise, there was not one person in front of me.

I went toward her with a huge smile on my face saying, "Louise, is this really happening?" She looked into my eyes and said, "Life *loves* you."

Wow.

It is indisputable. It is true. There is no doubt.

Life loves *me*, Wendy.

Every day, I hear her tell me: Life loves me.

Life loves you.

LOUISE HAY

While I was abusing drugs, food and shopping to numb my negativity, I perceived that my version of Authentic Expression was coming from my heart. In retrospect, I understand that it was, instead, from my wounded spirit. Being a rebel, I wreaked havoc on many lives, including my own. I was determined to do everything my way, no matter what. While I was authentic, it didn't compliment the other ingredients in my life.

A big part of my authenticity has always been evident in the creative and unique way I dress. Back then I needed to be seen. I made up that when people paid attention to me, they liked me, and then I felt better about myself. It was a vicious, and sometimes exhausting, cycle.

These days I know to rein it in. It can be an internal struggle when I'm hired to speak for organizations that may not appreciate my funky, artistic flair. If I put on a suit, they may like the way I look, but I will not feel like myself. If I wear my hippy chic clothes, they may not be able to hear what I'm there to say. Try liking yourself first, and share that genuineness with others. This is the most scrumptious combination.

Honoring this ingredient helped me find a happy medium with outfits that feel natural and comfortable, as well as an inner voice that supports my professional sassiness. I am more relaxed in my skin and make a bigger impact on the group. It is true—I have tried it both ways. Authentic expression always wins, and I do *not* wear pantyhose.

You be you is the best recipe for fulfillment. Be true to yourself, and meet others halfway when you must. Just don't disappear into their expectations.

"We are not here to fit in, be well balanced, or provide exempla for others. We are here to be eccentric, different, perhaps strange, perhaps merely to add our small piece, our little clunky, chunky selves, to the great mosaic of being. As the gods intended, we are here to become more and more ourselves."

– JAMES HOLLIS

ART BY REBECCA THURMAN

To live a life that you are madly in love with, you have to like who you are even when your life does not look lovable. When I was poisoning myself with drugs, bad thoughts, amoral actions and unhealthy relationships, self-love was nearly impossible.

Using affirmations, I was slowly able to change my thoughts from, "I am not good enough, nobody loves me and I am a loser," to "I am perfect as I am and I am loved." Even though I didn't yet truly believe it, my yearning to believe it drove me, over time, to trust it. I came to KNOW in my heart that I am perfect as I am, no matter what I think.

Often, my newfound thoughts were not strong enough to overcome the vicious cycle I was living. Because I had repeatedly hurt the people closest to me, it was difficult for them to even glimpse the excellence I was beginning to see in myself. The more I was told I was screwed up, the more attention I put there. I was confused and did not know who to believe—myself or them.

This plethora of mixed messages is a common challenge. My youngest sister, Erica Burns, illustrates this common dilemma with:

Ode to Joy

When I was twelve, I decided that I wanted to play the saxophone. I took a band class at my elementary school for two years, and was the only one of my friends to carry my instrument with me to high school. I played for one more year before deciding I was way too cool to be in the band.

Eighteen years later, I look back at that girl who gave up something she enjoyed and I shake my head at her. So here I am, fresh into my thirtieth year, trying to pick up where I left off with something I enjoyed so much in my youth. I am taking saxophone lessons at a local studio with a teacher who is my age, but who never put down his horn.

"Do what you need to help it all come back to you," he told me at our first lesson.

"Can I call you Mr. Lewis? That was the name of my sixth grade band teacher," I told him. Though I've only resorted to calling him Mr. Lewis a couple of times, I was pleased to find how quickly my musical knowledge has come back to me. And what is more amazing is that I look forward to going home after work to practice, which was something I dreaded when I was twelve.

The other night, practicing Beethoven's "Ode to Joy," a song I played at my very first band recital in sixth grade, the notes moved through my fingers and out of the saxophone as easily as they did then. I had just as much satisfaction in playing them for myself as I did then, in front of a roomful of proud parents.

As we get older, we learn that what others think of us is less important than what we think. I had always been disappointed in myself for giving up the saxophone, but I feel a sense of accomplishment now. I haven't mastered any skills, but I allow myself to find joy in the music that I'm making. It's never too late to create that for yourself.

Thoughts create feelings, feelings create actions, and actions, well, that is from where the results come. Trudging through the day-to-day duties of life, what we truly pine for can become misplaced. Instead of being a visionary—putting attention on your dreams, desires and possibilities, you spend more time being a "*whatisionary,*" mired in "what is." A visionary is spending valuable time and energy focusing on what they want for their lives. It's a law of the universe that we get more from where our attention is focused. Unless your life is exactly as you want it to be, it's prudent to spend more time in your role as a visionary.

So many people struggle with self-image, especially when trying to obtain and sustain their ideal body weight. They start this program, then that one, and spend lots of time and money to lose or gain.

As a *whatisionary*, your thoughts keep you focused on staying exactly where you are.

I am fat.

I am out of shape.

I need to lose weight.

These judgments keep you stuck. As you gently, yet persistently, shift to imagining how you wish to look, you will begin to feel the hope and the possibility of being healthy. Partner that with positive affirmations and your actions will shift. You'll make smarter food choices. Your exercise regime will support your dream and you will move closer and closer to your ideal weight. You'll choose a salad over a burger, and you'll take a walk instead of watching yet another rerun of *Friends*. Your vision becomes the catalyst for inspired action.

Sometimes I waffle between being a visionary and whatisionary, which was evident when I decided to quit smoking cigarettes. That habit was the antithesis of my Authentic Expression, so I began to see myself as a healthy person. The affirmation I used was "I prefer health." I would repeat that to myself, (I prefer health) even as I stood outside (I prefer health) in the freezing cold, (I prefer health) smoking (I prefer health). I saw what health would look like for me. I knew the positive impact that stopping this delicious, yet disgusting habit would have on my relationship with Matt. (I prefer health) There I was, smoking and affirming. (I prefer health) After about four months, (I prefer health) I was smoking less. Five months in, (I prefer health) I had stopped smoking (I prefer health) once and for all. Six years later, (I prefer health) I still crave one every now and again, yet lean right back into my affirmation of "I prefer health" and let the craving pass. (I prefer health) When I changed my thinking, the shift happened.

I prefer health.

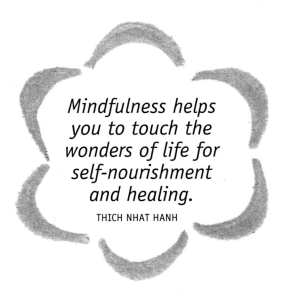

Mindfulness helps you to touch the wonders of life for self-nourishment and healing.

THICH NHAT HANH

It is time for you to create a part of your Authentic Expression ingredient by writing affirmations that represent your genuine self.

Affirmations always begin with I am . . . I can . . . I will . . . some way of claiming what you desire. If you can easily fill in the blank with something positive, do so. If something negative comes up, this is the time to flip it around to make it positive.

For example, if the thought that comes to your mind is that you're fat, and your desire is to be thin or healthy, ponder what you can shift to be more positive.

I am open to health and vitality.

I make healthy eating choices.

Water is my beverage of choice.

Our subconscious mind hears and responds to what we want. What do you really want?

My Authentic Expression affirmation is:

_____

_____

_____

_____

Diane felt it in her bones when she realized that her job in corporate America was not satisfying, and she came to me for coaching. She identified her purpose and passions, and over time, accepted the qualities of her authentic expression as a healer. She was deliberate and consistent in her vision, as she changed the ingredients in her recipe. Today, Diane loves her new career and her joy-filled life.

Conscious creation is the stock of all of these recipes. Knowing yourself, your strengths, your skills, your mission, moves you onto a path of realness. You decide how to show up: how you look, how you communicate, what you do. Life happens, so there will be times when you're not 100 percent in control, but still, it's your life; you get to choose. Stay in alignment with who you are, and your Joy Factor will make a positive impact on everyone around you.

So who are you?

Your personal values are at the core of your being, and these must to be present for your recipe to work and taste really good. If this ingredient is missing, you may be the only one who knows, yet others may sense that something is not quite right.

Your values give the unique flavor that others love about you. Unlike your passions, which evolve over time, personal values usually remain the same. They are the compass that gives you a genuine approach to a fulfilling life.

ART BY EMILY LOVVORN

My nine-year-old niece Emily is transparent, lighting up about animals, dancing and singing, being on camera, winning, and telling people what to do. She is creative, compassionate, and a natural leader who loves to have fun. She also loves to be tickled and laugh for hours. It is so easy to see her values. As she identifies and integrates them, her Joy Factor will only grow stronger.

She wrote for me, *"If you need joy, where should you go? You need to go to the Joy Factor! Where happiness happens! World peace, thank you Joy Factor."*

Unsolicited. Out of the mouth of babes. Brilliance!

Emily inspired this yummy childhood exercise:

CHILDHOOD YUMMIES

- Find pictures of you at a variety of ages, from five to twelve.
- Reconnect with those delightful beings and remember what brought you most alive at that age. Was it arts and crafts, traveling, journaling, playing? Uncover those yummies and make a list. On my list of yummies, there is:

  1. Coloring
  2. Singing
  3. Performing
  4. Anything with Play-Doh
  5. Going to the park
  6. Playing dress up

- Only choose things you remember loving, the things that brought you most alive.
- Notice the things that you think you *should* have loved or things that you wish you loved. Leave out the things that your parents wanted you to love, unless these were inviting to you.

PHOTO BY OANA HOGREFE

Look at your list and

1. Acknowledge the qualities that you brought with you from childhood.

2. If they are missing, get curious about how you can find and integrate them.

3. If they are present, it is time to peel the juicy fruit and get to the core of the yummy.

For instance, if creativity is one of the yummies, then how can you be more creative?

If hanging out with friends was on the list, how can you be more social?

These qualities are clues to your values, to what must be present in your life to experience the most joy and fulfillment.

List your Top Five Childhood Yummies:

1. _____

2. _____

3. _____

4. _____

5. _____

If you think that it will be hard to uncover your values, then it will be. If you intend that it will be easy, so be it. Wayne Dyer says, *"Our intention creates our reality."*

You'll find your values exactly where you find things that are most important to you, in your heart. When you look for these essential ingredients in your head, you can trip on those pesky "shoulds." From your heart, your values will bubble up.

Then ask yourself, what are the things that you must always have in your cupboard? These are akin to those comfort foods that make you feel the best. A few of my core values are creativity, adventure, laughter, contribution, learning and family. There are many facets of each of these, and when they are present, my Joy Factor is strong. I am fulfilled and productive.

In 2009, I was asked to be the incoming president for the Business Association in my city. My first thoughts were about all of the work, responsibility and stress that this volunteer position could bring, and the view did not look so great. As I shifted from the head-centered logic to my heart, the view was totally different. Yes, this opportunity would bring me more work and responsibility, but it would also give me an opportunity to honor my core values. Based on this, the decision was not a no-brainer; it came from my brain and heart—the perfect combination.

> *Remember always that you have not only the right to be an individual; you have an obligation to be one. You cannot make any useful contribution in life unless you do this.*
>
> ELEANOR ROOSEVELT

Parents and teachers expect high school seniors to already know their life path. This surprises me, and seems like lot of pressure for a teenager. Many of my adult friends, in their forties and fifties, still don't know what they want to be. Because of my life experience, I advocate for some kids to first attend the University of Life, from which I received my CHB: I am a Compassionate Human Being, and share this degree with pride. The break in formal education allowed me to consider what I wanted to contribute to the world. Part reflection and part exploration; sometimes consciously and other times not, the time let me glimpse my right path.

Too many people are meandering or floundering, creating a little of this and a little of that; dealing with a difficult economy, uncertain how to proceed; somewhat enjoying the journey, or not. It is often challenging to even figure out where to begin.

Look at the qualities of people you admire. Do you have the seeds of the next Martin Luther King, Jr. germinating? Maybe a little bit of Oprah or Emeril? Some are here for a world-changing purpose, others for something more tame or mainstream. Whatever mark you are here to leave, you must identify what is important to you. Passions are the breadcrumbs that lead us to our purpose in life. Our values are how we honor our passions. Consciously using these together in your recipe is a powerful combination.

In Estelle Reiner's obituary, the *New York Times* said she "delivered one of the most memorably funny lines in movie history." Mrs. Reiner was actor and director Rob Reiner's mother, and the movie was *When Harry Met Sally*. The famous scene was in Katz's Delicatessen, where Sally was teaching Harry that women can, in fact, fake "it."

"I'll have what she's having."

When you find people with qualities you admire, taste them. Integrate those qualities or values if they add flavor and substance to your recipe.

Colleague, wise woman, lover of all people, places and things, Sandra Kellim shares:

He Was "That" Guy

This was the guy who volunteered to help families in Africa, taught autistic children, cheerfully did dishes and stirred the soup when he was over for dinner. He was naturally polite, kind and funny. I used to joke that he was so wonderful that when he smiled we had to protect our eyes from the sparkling reflection. We knew something fun was going to happen when he bounded through the door. He organized the night that a bunch of kids, including my daughter, slept in a car piled on top of each other like puppies waiting for the annual REI sale to begin. They stocked up on the gear they needed to go out and experience nature at its finest.

Once, when she was describing him to me, my daughter said, "Mom, he was 'that' guy for me." He was the guy who showed her what it was like to be in a truly safe relationship. He held her hand gently, opened her car door, brushed the hair from her eyes and looked at her with such kindness and respect that I will always be grateful to him. He set the bar high.

He passed away in a rock climbing accident. Time has passed and we are still trying to make sense of it. He had a beautiful relationship with God and this comforts us all.

He embraced life with a ridiculous amount of enthusiasm and joy. The life he lived reminds me to be present and enjoy the simple stuff. I appreciate the opportunity to laugh loud, sing badly and contemplate the clouds in the sky. My daughter, who is slowly healing, feels the same way. She has made changes in her life so that she is really doing what she loves most and not wasting a single second. She has said that she wants to live her life in a way that will make him proud. Once again, I am grateful.

Let us not look back in anger or forward in fear, but around in awareness.

JAMES THURBER

While writing my first draft, I was reading a book from a speaker I shared the stage with at *The Prosperity Expo* in Florida in 2009. *Winning in Life Now* by Michelle Prince teaches people how to break through to a happier self. Our perspectives are so similar that, I thought, "oh yes, that is a great point and I should weave it into my story." The minute I heard myself think *should*, I glimpsed my ego. I feared that my concepts were not good enough, so I had better add some of this and some of that. I had to distinguish if this was coming from a feeling of abundance or lack, and was it the voice of my inner critic. In contrast, when it comes from my desire to contribute, then it is in alignment with authentic expression.

Not only did I gain inspiration from her book, I decided to have other people contribute their recipes to my Joy Factor approach. A lot of the essays and stories you are reading come from my Joy Factor blog. The unique views expressed by my Joy Posse, the collective of writers on the site, are a compliment to my take on creating a joyful life. My value of community is fully expressed by having others share their perspectives as is seen in the next essay from my beautifully authentic sister, Erica Burns:

Open Hearts and Open Minds

My yoga teacher tells us to check our egos at the door: "Don't compare yourself to others in the class, and don't force yourself into something that's not good for your body," she insists. "Lift your chest and open your heart," she advises during Eagle Pose. And so I do as she instructs. Drop my ego and open my heart— what sound advice! And though it seems it should be common sense, we need those reminders.

I often find that I compare myself to others, which seems odd since I am quite happy with who I am. In doing that, I find that I close my head and heart off to people as a result of my own judgment. That is the antithesis of what my sage of a yoga teacher preaches. In checking my ego at the door, I am not passing judgment on myself or others. In opening my heart, I am making room for the warmth of those around me, and most importantly, the love that I have to give myself. It's imperative to love ourselves before we can fully love others.

> *It's like the chicken or the egg: which comes first—an open heart or an open mind? Whichever comes first, the other is sure to follow, and both will lead us down the road to an open soul.*

Leave your ego at the door, open your heart and take a stab at writing five of your values. Think back over your Childhood Yummies and the qualities you admire in others.

1. _____

2. _____

3. _____

4. _____

5. _____

Shameless plug for professional coaching. If you want to go deeper in uncovering and aligning with your values, contact me or find another professional coach in your area.

Pay attention if you're adding things into your recipe because you think you should, other than to make it delicious. "Should" and "authenticity" are like oil and water—they do not blend. There is nothing worse for a recipe than a watered-down ingredient.

Of course, there are many factors that affect how we feel. Emotion is the measuring tool of sincere, real expression. Simply ask: am I being true to myself or not? Am I honoring the key values that represent my truth? Be honest, and adjust accordingly. Integrity may be a core value.

One of the most spot-on definitions of integrity comes from the Passion Test—the ability to be as true to yourself as you are to others and be as true to others as you are to yourself. Each day you have the opportunity to realign with what truthfulness is for you.

PHOTO BY OANA HOGREFE

Bernadette shares this perspective on integrity and Authentic Expression:

What Does It Really Mean to be Authentic?

A lot of people hate labels, but for me, it sometimes helps me understand a person. If they are genuine

about it, it can help someone express who they are—
quickly.

As a lesbian hippie of sorts, some of my friends
were surprised to learn that I enjoy Christian music.
Regardless of beliefs, the message is positive and the
music itself makes me feel good. Seven years ago, my
partner and I went to see Christian singer/songwriter,
Jennifer Knapp play at the Tabernacle in Atlanta. The
audience was a very different crowd from us, and we
expected a laid-back musical show. We were pleasantly
surprised when this tattooed rocker came out and enter-
tained us with the passion and presence that we didn't
pick up on her CD. We had a new respect for Jennifer as
she expressed her "authentic self."

After that concert, Jennifer didn't release any new
music. There were no tour dates and her website was
dormant for years. Fast forward to a few months ago,
my partner discovered that Jennifer Knapp was playing
at Eddie's Attic in Decatur. We had to go to satisfy our
curiosity. Turns out, she spent the past several years
disconnecting from the Christian commercial music
scene and discovering more about herself while exploring
Australia. On stage seven years later, we witnessed even
more passion and a deeper connection to her music.
Jennifer still has strong faith, but her beliefs have
broadened to embrace all people and the incredible
world around her.

I am amazed that when a person discovers more
about who they are and what brings them joy, the
expression of that and how they impact the world is

extremely powerful. I am on that journey myself, and am finding greater satisfaction when I make decisions that are in sync with my authentic self. How about you—what song are you waiting to release?

For many years I sang a dirge of pain and suffering. When the time came to rewrite my song, I was eager, yet scared. The hardest thing I have ever done was tell the people closest to me that I had been abusing prescription pain pills for thirty years. I was terrified of how they would respond, but living in integrity meant that they needed to know. They did not stop loving me. They did not leave me. Quite the opposite—they listened, cried with me . . . they opened their hearts and supported me in getting help. There is power in honesty and vulnerability and expressing oneself wholeheartedly.

Julia Murchison and I have laughed and learned together for twenty-one years. This is her recipe for joy.

Awesome Friends

My go-to ingredient for a joyous life is my awesome friends. They love me unconditionally and listen to my story without judgment, providing the words I need to hear to get back into my groove. Sometimes I just verbalize my issues. Hearing them, I recognize what direction I need to take.

In January of 2011, I left an unfulfilling job to go back to a career that I enjoyed prior to relocating to a very small town: massage and healing. I was ready for change and consistent income. Doing work that did not satisfy my heart and soul had caused stress-related health issues, yet leaving behind a steady paycheck and paid insurance was a huge and terrifying step. My joy was worth more, and I moved forward with my dream.

I felt elation in my new business, yet attracting customers was more challenging than I expected. Beginning this same type of business before in a bigger city was never this difficult. I didn't have the long-standing connections here and my spiritual viewpoints are counter to the local fundamental philosophies. Many of my deep-seated fears came up around finances, being accepted, being good enough and feeling worthy. I encountered many dark days during that year. Actively reaching out to my friends for the emotional support I needed, they were there to carry and cheer me on. I used the insights and tools they provided to work through issues as they came up.

This path was not the one I envisioned when I opened my business, yet it allowed me the opportunity to put things in perspective and choose what is really most important. I know deep in my soul that everything will turn out alright. It always does.

In moments of despair when you cannot see past your own limitations, allow the grace of your friends to elevate your life to a much better place.

My friends are the key ingredients in my Joy Factor recipe.

When you're making choices that are out of integrity with your passions, values and promises you made to yourself, feeling selfish is a red flag. Putting others first for fear of what they think is like cooking your recipes in an oven whose temperature gauge does not work—things cook too fast or too slow. Either way, it is never just right. I'm not saying that it is always all about you, but it starts with what is right for you.

"Life unexamined, is not worth living."
– DEMOCRITUS

"Now pitching for the Atlanta Braves, Jake Lovvorn."

We said this to him often when my nephew Jake was still in the womb. It's no surprise that he is an excellent baseball player, a left-handed pitcher, now fifteen years old, who wants to play professional baseball. We are certain that if he continues to focus on his goal, and does the best he can at school and for his team, he has a great chance to pitch for the Braves someday.

No matter how well Jake performs, his dad sees room for improvement, and Eric regularly takes him to the batting cages. His mom is the opposite, reminding him of what he did right. If our lives were always spent looking at what else we needed to do to be stronger, more successful, happier or more prosperous, without acknowledging our accomplishments both large and small, it would be hard to enjoy the journey.

Robert Holden suggests that looking for happiness is like missing the boat. He asks in his *Happiness Now* calendar, "What is your definition of a happy life? Are you living it? Think carefully about this because your definition of happiness will influence every other significant decision in your life."

Using Authentic Expression in your recipe starts with the decision to be authentic, then clarifying your authentic expression.

VIRTUAL VISIONING EXERCISE

See yourself ten years from now. Imagine yourself as gorgeous as you are going to be. Take a look inside at the essence of who you are. Weave in the yummies, your values, and *voilá*, you see yourself as you want to be. Create a visual expression of the future you. Place words and pictures from magazines on a piece of paper that express your ideal qualities, the ones that represent your Authentic Expression. You may want to use a technique called scripting to write, as if it has already happened, about that future. This journaling exercise will give you more clarity on the qualities of your future self.

This essay is another contribution from Bernadette, long-time journal writer and scripter.

Scripting for Joy

I'm not much for quiet meditation. I prefer the active kind where I am cycling or hiking, either by myself or thinking through something out loud with a friend. I'm not sure if that's right or wrong, but I certainly get more epiphanies and enjoyment from my version.

I've also been a big journaler all my life. Writing helps me process things. A few years ago, I learned about scripting from teacher and motivator Joyce Rennolds. It's pretty simple: as you write or re-read what you want, you feel the sense that you are experiencing it. It's an amazing way to leverage the Law of Attraction for positive change, and it is an active form of meditation.

Scripting precipitated a big decision to invest in mountain cabins with my sister. Scripting drove my journey to get me to those mountains full-time. And scripting continues to shape my future as I envision the next change in my life.

Recently I sat down to script about my future. I took a section of my current day at work that I already enjoy and built on it in my imagination. I love the quiet morning by myself at the coffee shop preparing for the day. I love the smell of fresh ground beans, the "coffee house" music and setting up processes that will help me serve people quickly and efficiently during the morning shift. I love seeing the regulars and having their drinks or bagels started as they walk in the door. I love catching up with new friends and sharing the first moments of their day.

I took that scenario and expanded it, adding specific elements that would make it even better. I know that the world is at work crafting the details. And it brings me joy to imagine it, even if it doesn't play out exactly as I expected. Scripting helps me discover the essence of what makes me happy, and sets things in motion to bring more of it into my life.

As you start to use this ingredient in your recipe, you will feel more alive, more connected to who and what you are meant to be, and your energy level will increase. It is important to stay connected to your Big Why. Why is it that you want to increase your Joy Factor, anyway? In *Think and Grow Rich,* Napoleon Hill says that when you unearth your burning desire, or what is most important to you, you move toward that desire.

The more I stayed connected to my Big Why, adding value to millions of lives, even when it felt hard and I thought I couldn't write or rewrite another word, the vision moved me forward better than a double espresso.

You are here to live your best life. Continue to move forward and craft "the real thing."

*The truly important
things in life—
love, beauty, and one's
own uniqueness—
are constantly
being overlooked.*

PABLO CASALS

What is Your Recipe for Authentic Expression?_____

_____

_____

_____

_____

_____

_____

_____

_____

_____

_____

_____

_____

_____

_____

_____

_____

_____

_____

_____

_____

_____

_____

_____

_____

_____

Self-Care is like keeping your fountain full.

WENDY WATKINS

126

Chapter 6

Feed Yourself First

PHOTO BY WENDY WATKINS

Chapter 6

Feed Yourself First

Imagine this: you're on a plane and one of the worst things (besides running out of peanuts) happens. The oxygen masks drop. You remember the flight attendant saying to put one on yourself first and then on your child. You know this is the right thing to do, however your impulse is to take care of your child first. If you can't breathe, how can you take care of others?

The concept of Self-Care, the third ingredient of the Joy Factor, can be a real conundrum. In theory, most agree that if you take care of yourself first, you have more to give to those you care about. When it comes to action, the decision is challenging. Think of the times that you have had to make that choice: to take care of yourself or somebody else.

Do I take that yoga class or go to my kid's soccer game?

Do I tell my boss that I will finish the project over the weekend or attend my kid's weekend scouting jamboree?

Do I join my best friends for a girls night out, or do I head to the movies with my family?

Me or them? Them or me? Is there a right answer?

As a Conscious Creator, you choose. Ask yourself: what will support me in having more happiness and bliss?

Sometimes we use our MSU to make stuff up that is really not true. In the arena of Self-Care, it happens a lot. Mom's make up the notion that their kids always have to have what they want first. Now, I'm not a mom, except to my sweet dogs, Abbey Road and Eli, but I still experience "mommy guilt" from time to time. I want to go to the gym and they need a walk. Which is most important? You may be thinking that in this case, I should do what I want to do for me and not worry about the dogs. I love those dogs like any member of my family, so the choice is hard.

I feel good when I uncover what I know I need to do for myself first and act on it, so both my vibration and Joy Factor increase. Then, I am fully available to be there for others, and we all enjoy the doggie stroll.

Have you ever been around a beautiful desktop fountain when it is out of water? They make a heinous noise. Self-Care is like keeping your fountain full; the sight and sound of the flowing water brings me peace and serenity. What are you like when you fill your fountain? On the flip side, what is your life like when that gorgeous fountain of yours is empty?

The full fountain is akin to our quest for balance. Are we ever really balanced? When I was a little girl, my sister Lisa and I loved spending time on the seesaw. It was so much fun to go up and down. Sometimes, we would both stop and put our feet on the ground and "be balanced." That would only last for a minute and then we would want to go up and down again. Life will always offer opportunities that shift the scales. I propose a new perspective: you're either moving towards balance or away from it.

Each day is full of delicious things to achieve. Some days I'm able to get everything done, and others there are "leftovers" for me to enjoy from earlier in the week. Things on the to-do list can slip by unnoticed. I feel more peace and trust, knowing that everything is happening in divine order. It's okay if something is not checked off on my list. My internal barometer lets me know when I am on-purpose and energized, and if I'm doing my best.

In *The Four Agreements*, Don Miguel Ruiz says to "keep in mind that your best is never going to be the same from one moment to the next. Everything is alive and changing all the time, so your best will sometimes be high quality, and other times it will not be as good."

As I strive to check things off of my list every day, I'm easy on myself. If I'm not in a place of expansion, of feeling good, feeling alive, then it may not be the time to move forward on a particular activity.

Over the last couple of weeks, my plate has been very full with many tasty things to accomplish and there have been lots of those "leftovers." As I was "cleaning out the fridge," I noticed some of these items were on the edge of stinky and really needed to be done. I was at the breaking point, that edge where I knew that if I did not shift my energy, completing those tasks was going to make me cranky. Part of me wanted to plow through and get it done, but I knew that if I did, when Matt was done at work, neither he nor I would love the woman to whom he came home. I took a breath, changed my clothes and went for a bike ride. An hour of doing something that fed my spirit shifted my mood, and later that evening I finished the last items on the list, without dread or resentment.

A dishonest yes is a no to yourself.

BYRON KATIE

There are four aspects of Self-Care, cornerstones to give you a strong foundation of balance: physical, mental, emotional and spiritual.

PHYSICAL

Over the years, personal fitness challenges have kept my focus on physical self-care.

In 2001, I did the three-day, sixty mile Avon Walk for Breast Cancer, and raised over $3,500 for breast cancer research. Completing a 10K was my target for 2008, and I ran (well, walked and ran) the Peachtree Road Race. Then, in 2010, I did a century bicycle ride to celebrate my forty-eighth birthday. Having this type of target supports me in both balance and self-care. It gives me structure and focus so that this important part of my recipe does not fade into the background.

The physical aspect of your life includes exercising, eating well, drinking enough water and loving your body. This is not new information. What is fresh will be the inspired actions you take to gain different results. Strict goals tend to de-motivate. What does motivate is a compelling personal challenge aligned with your goals and values— your Big Why—which allow you to enjoy the benefits you reap.

The specific activities may change over the years, so allow your choices to evolve. Notice what is satisfying to your Self-Care palette. Here is a sampler of physical activities, large and small, that may spin your wheels and move you into action:

- Join thousands of people in events from running marathons to riding centuries with Team in Training.
- Be the catalyst that gets you and your friends off of the couch and walking in parts of your city that you have not seen before.
- Rescue a dog. They love walks. This is good for your heart and soul.

- Attend an innovative class that gets you into your body, such as pole-dancing, Zumba, yoga or Pilates.
- Take a healthy cooking class. Experiment with vegan, vegetarian or gluten free foods.

Physical nurturing supports both the emotional and mental aspect of your Joy Factor. When you use a little salt and pepper, it brings the other flavors alive in your dish. When you take care of your body, you feel good. When you feel good, it is easier to think good thoughts (mental) and feel good (emotional). When your physical focus is off target, it may be attention to your emotions, mind or spirit that brings you back towards balance.

*You are unique,
and if that is
not fulfilled,
then something
has been lost.*

MARTHA GRAHAM

MENTAL

One of the most challenging things to do as you begin to deliberately craft a delicious life is to uncover what makes you feel good.

Thomas hired me to show him how to become a conscious creator. The first thing we did was to inventory the things that Thomas did on

133

a daily basis. From there we decided what needed to be adjusted to support him in raising his Joy Factor.

He was living a delightful life filled with great friends, family and fun. The one thing standing in the way of enhancing his joy was his habit of watching the news every morning and evening, which dampened his ability to feel good. Soon after eliminating news from his daily diet, Thomas' vibration lifted, elevating his thoughts and feelings.

Those thoughts are the basis of the mental balance of self-care, which are the result of what you are read, watch or hear. You get sucked in, and the next thing you know, your vibration is low and dull, dull, dull.

Bad news feeds fear and doubt about things we cannot control. If you want to be current on world events, by all means, surf to CNN. com or MNN.com, or ask others who can keep you informed.

Juliette Mansour, photographer, graphic diva, doggie lover and cyclist, shares how she gets rid of the Inner Killjoy.

Inner Killjoy

See if this sounds familiar: Life is coasting along like a souped-up tricycle when out of nowhere: CRASH! You're knocked over by a nasty twist of fate—a little monster I call, the inner killjoy, your own personal party pooper either you unwittingly create or pick up elsewhere like a germ. Violently, it drags you through unhappy chaos. It tends to happen in threes, if you haven't noticed. Before you know it, you're angry, frantic, or worse, you've taken it out on someone dear.

One day I met up with my inner killjoy after a prolonged, appreciated absence. Round two with this insipid force and I wondered, "Can I not catch a break?" Then, "These things happen in threes! There's one more coming!" That last thought ushered in an escalation.

Joy disappeared along with sanity, and I wanted them back!

Two things I learned about its wrath:

#1: Flailing about won't rescue me.

#2: Most times, neither will thinking it through.

There is however, a power from within that can, a formula for keeping my joy. The formula and the prevention are the same: dedicated quiet time.

Most start their day off with a shower followed by the morning news, a little breakfast and a mad dash to work. For me, it's meditation first. Meditation or quiet time all accomplish the same purpose. It inserts a sanity buffer between getting up and getting out the door. It preps the mind with a spiritual shower. As I heard someone say, we take a shower to wash off street muck from our bodies, so why wouldn't we cleanse our minds as well?

Taking a daily spiritual shower makes energy ripe for a higher frequency. Even five minutes of dedicated stillness puts my thoughts in "time out" and gives me the ability to rest in that sweet spot where energy expands. Over time, it offers indescribable peace and connection. It allows for all that is. And the best part: I get to keep my joy.

What are you feeding your mind? Are you reading positive things? Are you spending your time with positive people? There are a variety of things that will support you in choosing balance. Books of daily affirmations, joke books, inspirational websites and so much more.

"Thoughts become things...choose the good ones," says Mike Dooley, founder of the Adventurers Club and author of the wonderful *Notes from the Universe*. Choose them wisely.

Worry never robs tomorrow of its sorrow, it only saps today of its joy.

LEO BUSCAGLIA

EMOTIONAL

The emotional aspect of Self-Care is often overlooked. For many years, I made up that feeling would be too scary and painful. From the outside it wasn't obvious that internally, I was suffering and struggling for peace, balance and happiness. I stuffed those painful feelings and carried around a matched set of emotional baggage by taking pills, overeating, smoking cigarettes, shopping, etc. to numb my emotions. These bags coordinated with everything I was feeling (or not feeling) and seemed natural to schlep everywhere I went.

After thirty years, even I couldn't handle my erratic behavior any longer. For no reason, I would "blow up" like a volcano, leaving myself and the people around me perplexed and damaged. This is the fallout of being disconnected from our emotional essence.

I'll always remember a powerful session with my coach, Jeanine Mancusi, co-director of Lucid Living, when I began to feel my authentic expression. As I felt the thrill and hope in that moment, I also witnessed my urge to deaden that expansive emotion.

My coaching sessions were on the phone, so the walk to the fridge was easy. I grabbed a big spoon on the way and began to stuff those feelings of power . . . by eating yogurt. It took about two minutes to realize what I was doing, and I told on myself. Jeanine and I laughed about it as I put the yogurt back in the refrigerator. A few minutes later, once more, I was reaching for the yogurt.

It can take a while to break our old habits. Are you allowing yourself to feel? And feel deeply? Do you know how?

The search for happiness and joy outside of ourselves is evidence that we don't really know how to feel and express emotions, so there is a lot of opportunity to use this ingredient. All emotions are included—the highs and the lows. Not only was I afraid to feel what I thought were "bad" emotions, I did not know how to feel the "good" ones.

Once I stopped abusing substances, my life took a dramatic turn for the better. It would change the world if people knew that it was okay to feel whatever is coming up, and to know that you won't be stuck in that feeling forever.

"How are you doing?" or "How are you feeling?" are common questions of greeting. Most often, the answers are predictable: "fine," "I'm doing well," or "I'm having a bad day." There are hundreds of words besides "good" and "bad" to express how we actually feel. Language, or word choice, connects you to your emotions in a way that you may have never imagined. It can be an authentic expression, or it can be an affirmation.

Feelings and emotions are just that. They come from a thought and the thought can be changed. Neither good nor bad, they're just feelings. If you are sensing worry or doubt, it is just an emotion. If you are feeling hatred, that is what you are feeling. The experience of that hatred is going to feel constricting, yet it is not a bad thing, unless you label it such and act on it. If you feel the hatred, really let yourself go there, you can then move up the scale to feeling better.

In *Ask and It is Given* by Abraham-Hicks, they share their Emotional Guidance System, a list of twenty-two words that range from high vibration feelings (joy, passion, love) to lower vibration emotions (insecurity, fear). They liken it to a scale with a wide range in between the feelings. As you explore the depth and width of each word, you become proficient in guiding your emotional journey.

When Matt makes a pot of chili that's too spicy, we add more tomatoes. When you are having a rough day, add more love and understanding. The tide goes in and the tide goes out; we will have feelings that move us toward expansion and ones that cause us to constrict. To feel deeply may not be easy, but it *can* lead to enhanced happiness and fulfillment.

Lucid Living and Abraham-Hicks have been instrumental in teaching me to replace the fear of feeling with trust. As with any new habit, it becomes easier with practice.

Here is a place to begin:

1. When you notice that you are feeling something, stop, and do your best not to judge it or numb it.

2. Identify the emotion. When you stop long enough and are familiar with the nomenclature, it will become second nature.

3. Remember, you will not be trapped here forever. A baby is a perfect example, moving effortlessly between joy, happiness, hunger, discomfort, fatigue, and then the baby laughs, cries or giggles, before it moves on.

4. Once you experience the emotion, express it. You can journal about it, talk to someone, or sing it. If the emotions are overwhelming, then find a professional to help.

The Emotional Guidance System is one place to find an emotional vocabulary, and there are a plethora of books and tools to help you evolve from being numb to being fully alive.

Think about something you love—a person, place or thing. Really put your attention there and notice how this makes you feel. Then think about something that you don't love. Now shift back and forth in this simple version of an emotional roller-coaster, between who/what you do, and don't, love. This practice becomes more comfortable and you won't be afraid of the highs or the lows of the expressive ride.

When you're having a rough day, accept it is as sign from the Universe to slow down, or rest. Think of it as the Universe's red or green light. When you come to a red light, you naturally stop. If you don't stop, you risk an accident or a ticket. Do you get upset that you have to stop at the red light? Usually not, it's just a rule of the road. It is the same for how you are feeling each day.

The next step is life changing—be gentle on yourself. When the negative self-talk says, "You *should* feel good; you *should* finish everything you need to get done today. What a slacker," simply turn the volume down. Or off. Be as kind as you would if your best friend was having a bad day.

My teachers Chris Attwood and Janet Bray Attwood, co-authors of *The Passion Test* shared this with me and it transformed the way I felt about having a "bad day." When you come to that proverbial red light, add compassion and acceptance. Give yourself permission to have this lower vibration.

Here is a simple example of what that may look like. You have plans to go to dinner with friends. You get home from work and realize that you really want to spend an evening alone.

You decide to honor yourself and reschedule the plans. Because you have chosen to surround yourself with people who love you, they understand and support you.

Now, here is where you choose to feel good or not. Do you stay home and beat yourself up for not going with your friends, or do you enjoy your evening on the sofa with pizza and a movie?

The Self-Care ingredient is powerful. Remember, not every ingredient goes in every recipe. When you are ready to use authentic feeling in your recipe, you know where to begin. When Matt wants to learn to cook something from another country, he will usually take a class or apprentice with someone. If Self-Care is a new skill, find the teacher or program to help you. In the meantime, become friends with your emotions. They will let you live life to the fullest.

PHOTO BY PAT THOMAS

SPIRITUAL

"Spiritual" could be God, the Universe, Source Energy—whatever it is you want to call it. My connection with Spirit is found when I slow down and am surrounded by nature, whether on a five-minute stroll, a thirty-minute walk or a five-hour bike ride. Some days I may not have time to spend outdoors, so I have "nature" in my home— lots of plants, flowers, rocks, shells and pictures of the gifts that Mother Nature has provided. I can look out my window and see the treetops, the sky, the sun and the birds. They remind me that I am linked to something bigger than myself.

When you get stuck in the minutia of your world; paying bills, feeding the kids and answering the plethora of emails and phone calls, step back and connect with Spirit. There are many ways to do this. This is your recipe; what would work for you? It could be spending time in nature, or visualizing, meditating, singing, dancing or connecting with the God of your choice.

We are shaped by our thoughts; we become what we think. When the mind is pure, joy follows like a shadow that never leaves.

BUDDHA

Juliette Mansour, Atlanta photographer, says it may be about:

Changing the Background Music

Music has an extraordinary way of healing, inspiring and creating ambiance but its biggest prowess is in the area of enhancing emotions and influencing creativity. I was raised on many genres of music that influenced my experiences with the guitar since learning to play at the age of nine. These experiences convinced me that we become more flexible both personally and outwardly when we fall in love with music.

The next time you watch a movie, focus on the background music. Watch how it influences your inter-

pretation of the plot. Think of your exercise play list and how it creates that extra burst of adrenaline at the gym. Listen to the sounds of nature and take note of how they affect your level of peace and openness. Then think about how your mood is altered when watching the news on T.V., dodging traffic while talking on the phone or at a crowded Walmart. What does this do to your creativity?

I believe music can remove the worst of creative blocks. I also believe that ingenuity and creativity return when there is less exposure to stressful or stagnant background noise.

So, if you want to bust open your writer's block, shift your artistic direction, or raise your Joy Factor, try changing the background noise. Listen to different types of music as you write, paint, or even cook. Then look at what you created and think about what you listened to at the time. You may be surprised at the results.

When you are in the flow and enjoying your day, take a few minutes to list three or four things that will raise your Joy Factor. Keep your list handy, so when you are having a less-than-great day, you will know what to do.

Chris Attwood, co-author of *The Passion Test*, shares this about using meditation to stay connected and joyful:

"Meditation has been my ritual for many years. I meditate twice a day; in the morning and evening. It provides a

wonderful anchor for my life. It begins the day on a good note and ends it in a good place. The other thing that happens is it creates the foundation on which my life has been built. It is a strong, stable foundation of inner wakeful-ness. Life becomes a conscious process. As consciousness increases, you notice your beliefs and passions. As you create conscious habits, such as consistently choosing in favor of your passions, you can more easily say no to the things that are not connected to what you love. It is about living a fully conscious life."

My spin teacher Kim, a wise and funny woman offers this:

Recipe for Joy

Sometimes you need to empty yourself and start anew. This can be achieved in a variety of ways—a hard workout, a yoga class, perhaps a bike ride: anything that will thoroughly clean your mixing bowl and utensils.

Begin adding only the choicest ingredients. GRATITUDE makes a delicious and substantial base. Add KINDNESS, as everyone you meet is carrying a heavy burden. FRIENDSHIP is invaluable to keeping elasticity in the batter.

An ACCURATE MEASURE is required for your PER-SPECTIVE, as it can easily become skewed and affect the outcome of your dish. A good dose of HUMOR is most delectable. LOVE and COMPASSION for yourself and others are two mandatory ingredients for a joyful life.

Be sure to throw in some spice to engage your brain—a good book, puzzle or something to TANTALIZE THE MIND.

It is essential to sift out any UNREALISTIC EXPEC-TATIONS, JUDGEMENT, JEALOUSY and WORRY, not to mention ANGER and NEGATIVE THINKING. Remembering what to leave out of your recipe is just as important as knowing what to include.

Mix the ingredients daily by engaging in some form of EXERCISE, like a brisk walk, bike ride or yoga class. This will keep the ingredients from settling.

It is imperative to allow the dough to REST. This PAUSE is best taken in the natural world. Taking time to SEE the moon, a caterpillar or an unusual flower are just a few ways to acknowledge the miracle of life, and provide that extra PATIENCE that is critical to the outcome of your special concoction.

There are some optional ingredients to liven up the recipe. If your taste buds need a hot and spicy twist, try adding something that truly SCARES you. If it is CALM you seek instead of adventure, consider adding a swing in a hammock or some time in a rocking chair.

Occasionally an ingredient may be added when you aren't looking. Do NOT toss the batch out and start anew. This is when CREATIVE cooking comes into play, for it is these unexpected ingredients, albeit oftentimes bitter, that make for a surprisingly delicious outcome.

Lastly, when you are ready to bake, be aware that ovens can be unreliable. You may not have total control over the temperature, so be prepared for your recipe to take a little longer than expected. In the end, take pride in what you have created, knowing it is the result of your exquisite handiwork. Don't be fooled by how it looks, for looks are often deceiving. Close your eyes and take a bite of this most nourishing dish. Chew slowly to savor every tiny bit.

Everyone's taste buds are unique, so feel free to tweak this to make your own mouth water.

Integrating any of the Self-Care ingredients into your recipe will not only lift your Joy Factor, but your intuition will grow stronger. The more you listen to those whispers, the more they will guide you.

Listening to my intuition led me to one of my favorite books about the sixth sense. I was at the library selecting books for Matt, a voracious reader who enjoys just about anything. As I perused the shelves, I picked up Char Margolis' book, *Discover Your Inner Wisdom: Using Intuition, Logic, and Common Sense to Make Your Best Choices*. I looked at it and thought, nah, I have a stack of books at home in the queue and I am here for Matt. I returned it to the shelf.

Then I giggled out loud, right there in the non-fiction section. For weeks I had been yearning to deepen my relationship with my intuition. There she was, tapping me on the shoulder, and I had ignored her. I went back to the shelf, picked up the book and recommitted to honoring my intuition. This is truly a conscious choice. The more I listen, the more she guides me.

My friend Jen and I scheduled a Thursday morning bicycle ride to Stone Mountain. I packed all of my gear, yet forgot to put air in my tires. I knew I should have checked them, but I wanted to be at her place on time. Off we went, and after about three miles, I hit a bump and phew: a flat tire. We looked at each other and laughed hard at our inexperience in changing tires. A fellow rider stopped and shared his tools, Jen changed the rear tire like a pro, and off we went.

It was a reminder to listen to my gut. The more I act on my intuition, the more she is there to support me, saving me time and energy. I can push her aside just like I can my Self-Care. I make up the excuse that I don't have time, or I have to do something for someone else, and then I get a "flat tire."

What is your intuition telling you now? Not sure? Hold the intention to connect with her, and listen.

A nice bicycle is quite an investment, and we waffled back and forth for almost a year before Matt bought Wasabi, my Trek road bike, as my birthday gift. I was seeing this purchase more as a cost, versus contributing to my Joy Factor until I admitted that Self-Care is priceless. When I do something good for me, it is going to feel good for others too.

Once we decided, there was a lightness and freedom in the house. Not because I was riding a bike that I loved, but because space was now free in our minds. Procrastinating about decisions can stagnate your Joy Factor.

Maryel Tomter, a loving woman and client in my Joy of Attraction coaching group, tells about knowing what you know.

Instant Morning Brew

2 Eyes shut

1 Very clear mind

5 Deep breaths inhaled beginning from your
toes and exhaled totally

1 Strong connection to the silence you hear
from inside your soul

Allow these ingredients to come together on their own
for as long as needed. Once done, the focus and clarity
will give you the energy and jolt to greet each day with
passionate success.

Taking care of yourself is a significant ingredient in your Joy Factor recipe. You may need to marinate like a fresh piece of tuna in wasabi dressing—it takes a while to get used to the flavor of raw fish—and you may need to start off with little bites. The cool thing is that your family, friends and coworkers will appreciate you more when you are happy and healthy. It may take them a minute to get used to it, but think of the example you are setting. What if your son, daughter, niece or nephew can learn this in their formative years? They can embrace the benefits of keeping their fountain full, and not have to retrain themselves after they learned to take care of others first.

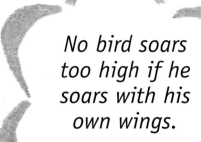

*No bird soars
too high if he
soars with his
own wings.*

WILLIAM BLAKE

What is Your Recipe for Self-Care? _____

_____

_____

_____

_____

_____

_____

_____

_____

_____

_____

_____

_____

_____

_____

_____

_____

_____

_____

_____

_____

_____

_____

_____

_____

_____

_____

PHOTO BY WENDY WATKINS

Chapter 7

Filling Your Cup

*A strategic plan for
optimism will keep
pessimism at bay.*

WENDY WATKINS

Chapter 7

Filling Your Cup

My sister Lisa is a runner. She sets up a program and does her best to honor it, knowing how many miles she needs to run each week to meet her end goal of a marathon or half marathon. I've been at the finish line when she completed several races with ease and grace, ready to join her in celebrating with her favorite treat, doughnuts.

On my journey to joy and bliss, I noticed a combination of good days, great days, not-so-great ones and some that were downright bad. Welcome to being human! I saw that when I chose to have an excellent day, I did. When I set my intentions for the day, my day was productive, fruitful and enjoyable. If I didn't make that deliberate decision, it might or might not be. I was susceptible to negativity and energy vampires—people who talk about the news, death and murder, a drop in the stock market, the forecast for rain, blah, blah, blah. They would suck my A-positive blood, and I'd walk away feeling drained, wondering why I wasn't having a good day.

In *Happy for No Reason*, which I consider to be a happiness bible, Marci Shimoff writes about the Happy 100. She worked hard to find one hundred truly happy people. After many interviews and surveys, asking, "Who is the happiest person you know?;" her tenacity and persistence led her to folks who were deeply and consistently happy. Unless it is your nature, you have to *decide* to be happy.

If you want to join the ranks of the likes of Michael J. Fox, Michelle Obama, Marci Shimoff, Martin Seligman, Robert Holden, Wendy Watkins and others, then I invite you to embrace the concept of Strategic Optimism. Strategic Optimism is an important piece to take lives from oy to joy! A plan for optimism is as compelling as ice cream on a hot day.

If you are a businessperson, you probably have a business plan. You may have a financial or savings plan for retirement. To become fit, you have a fitness course of action. These targets, combined with action steps, help you reach your goals.

I've often heard having a good plan is simple, yet not easy. What helps is having a step-by-step approach. Breaking down big agendas into bite-sized pieces, like creating a joyful, fulfilling and satisfying life, not only helps in enjoying the process, it increases the likelihood of success.

Neill Corporation is the largest Aveda distributor in the world. They are an innovative and forward thinking organization that embraces the Joy Factor concepts. I had the honor of being on the faculty of the Neill Quality College—a business program for salon owners. Much of the curriculum was based on the teachings of W. Edwards Deming, who believed that 96 percent of the time people fail because they don't know what to do. They didn't have a system, or a plan.

Creative beings may have a hard time with the mere thought of structure and strategy. This is *not* a plan that you have to follow by being exact and precise. This method is one that you hold loosely rather than tightly; that guides and supports you, rather than directs and stifles you. In fact, flexibility is essential. If an apple a day keeps the doctor away, then *a strategic plan for optimism will keep pessimism at bay.*

The dissatisfaction of store-bought tomatoes was my impetus to become an urban gardener. After attending a few classes and reading a book or two, Matt dug out a plot and I designed the perfect in-town growing space. The promise of tomatoes, cucumbers, peppers, squash and a variety of herbs delighted me, the birds and the squirrels. They showed up in mass when the seedlings went into the ground. My garden started with a clear-cut outline. As time, rain, drought and heat enveloped my space, I had to make adjustments. As everything (well, most things) started to grow, the parts of the garden I gave time and attention to shifted according to need. After the harvest, there was another adjustment in care; it was quite a process.

I enjoyed the beauty we cultivated, yielding to my original intention of fresh vegetables, yet working the ever-evolving strategy for my plot. In some areas, I did not pay attention to my original plan,

Imagination is the gateway to opportunity and unexpected blessings.

WENDY WATKINS

evidenced by our skimpy harvest. It was a good reminder that even with Strategic Optimism in place; things may not turn out as desired.

This turn of events had me shopping at our local farmers market for tomatoes more than expected that summer. When this happens, being flexible and unattached to specific results will keep your optimism in bloom.

My intrinsic nature is to be joyful and happy. At times, though, I struggle with low-level depression, and I alter my recipes those days. I work with an amazing herbalist who feeds my body just what it needs to work through those dips. She is a key component in my plan for cheerfulness. Just like flour and water need yeast to rise into dough, it is imperative for you and I to have a strategy for optimism.

Enjoy this delightful recipe created by Susan Powell—a client, mommy and body-care-worker extraordinaire.

Wonder-Bread

First sprinkle a loaf pan liberally with your **positive intention,** and preheat your oven to the perfect temperature for you.

In a small bowl, blend the dry ingredients: pour one packet of **inspired action** into 1½ cups of warm **desire.** Add a heaping Tbsp of **gratitude** and wait **patiently** for it to activate.

*In a separate bowl, stir the liquids: 3 cups of **faith** (preferably organic) with 2 Tbsp of **time for quiet reflection and meditation**.*

Add the wet ingredients to the dry ones and stir passionately until it all begins to stick together.

*Then pour the dough on to a surface also sprinkled with **positive intention** and begin to **play** with it. Keep **playing** until it **feels good**. The finished dough should feel smooth and springy and not be sticky.*

*Now wait **patiently** for the dough to rise. Don't worry; you don't have to figure out the details, God will take care of this step for you.*

Sit back and relax.

*When your loaf has doubled in size, give it a punch of **clarity**, and then **play** with it again. Add more **positive intention** as needed. If the dough gets too tough, you can sprinkle in a little more **desire**.*

*Now you have to wait patiently again—this recipe requires a LOT of **patience**.*

*Allow the dough to rise again, this should be **effortless**. Sometimes, there are factors that might cause your bread not to rise as well; if this happens to you, just practice **acceptance** and try again. If you place your loaf in a space that is warm and happy, it will rise better.*

Once the dough is just the way you like it, place it in the perfectly warmed oven to cook. Enjoy the delicious smell of your Wonder-Bread as it bakes. Cook until it's in the zone.

*Remove from oven, and serve warm with a pat of melted **appreciation**. If you're feeling particularly experimental, you can drizzle your slice with a **shift of perspective**. For true bliss, top with a healthy dose of **love of the process**.*

Strategic Optimism revolves around a hopeful and positive view of future outcomes. If you choose to see the good in things, happiness and joy become effortless.

As a conscious creator, you know that "life happens." Many situations and events are out of our control. The only true thing we have control of is how we react to the experience. With this ingredient, you will be focusing on a plan to help you lean toward the positive.

I have driven a convertible for the last twelve years. I love having the top down, music on and speedometer racing. Yes, Wendy Andretti has received a few tickets. If I sprinkled some Strategic Optimism into my recipe that day, chances are that the blue lights and siren behind me won't upset me as badly. Moreover, when I'm feeling upbeat, it is easier to notice the nudge from the Universe to ease my foot from the gas pedal. I slow down, but always keep the music turned up.

PHOTO BY WENDY WATKINS

The power of a gratitude-attitude is delicious and imperative for Strategic Optimism. Deborah Norville, in her book, *Thank You Power*, says that two small words, "thank you," can change your life, for it is not just about the words, but the mind-set. Being conscious about the yummy combination of your positive thoughts, feelings and actions will move you in the direction you want to go. It will not only make you feel better, Norville shares that studies show it will improve your health, optimism and resilience in tough times.

Now is the perfect time to enjoy a bowl of my Gratitude Gumbo.

Gratitude Gumbo

Grow where you are planted. *You are where you are in your life for a reason. When you remember that and go with the flow, it will be easier to express gratitude for what is, rather than focusing on what could be or what was.*

Reset your mindset. *When you notice that you're complaining or blaming, push the reset button, and notice what you are thankful for. It could be the car you are driving, the food you are eating or the house where you live—you get to choose. Keep track of these delicious nuggets by writing them in a gratitude journal.*

Accentuate the positive. *Where do you want to shine the light? On what is working, or what is not working? Choose what works and share that with others. They will thank you.*

Treat every day as a gift. *Unwrap it and find the wonder in the newness and possibility. Savor, and be thankful.*

Imagine the possibilities. *If you don't like what you are experiencing, use your thoughts to shift it. Imagination is the gateway to opportunity and unexpected blessings.*

Two words: "Thank you." Use them often. Say it not only with your words, but with your eyes and actions.

Unite with others. We are connected human beings who desire to be appreciated, loved and acknowledged. Act accordingly.

Delight in Mother Earth. Nothing enhances gratitude more than spending time in nature. You cannot help but feel thankful for the glorious sights, sounds and smells. Step outside today.

Enjoy the journey. Don't worry about getting there; because once you get there, it is time to go someplace else. Savor the everyday moments.

Using jalapeno peppers in salsa will certainly give it some heat, just as gratitude is a sure-fire way to an encouraging vision of future outcomes. Being thankful to someone for helping you will shift attention away from what doesn't work to what does. I still try to appreciate the police officer who writes the speeding ticket.

Gratitude is natural for me, and counting my blessings is a daily activity. Before I go to sleep, I write down at least five things for which I am thankful, and the things of which I am most proud. The sensation is more snuggly than my super-soft blanket, and it is surely better than thrashing myself for what I did not accomplish. I accept that my to-do list will never be done, so I celebrate even my smallest successes.

Another life-enhancing practice is appreciating the things you do not yet have, but affirm or desire. Sarah Ban Breathnach, in *Simple Abundance: A Daybook of Comfort and Joy*, reminds us that until we appreciate what we already have, we can't expect the Universe to send us more. Start with the seemingly simple things—a roof over your head, food in your refrigerator, your health, and the money you had to buy this book.

Another way is offered to you by Tricia Molloy, author of *Divine Wisdom at Work: 10 Universal Principles for Enlightened Entrepreneurs*.

Reflect on Success

1. *Number your page from 1–20 on the left margin of your paper.*

2. *Consider what you're most proud of this year, including family and friends, health, work, finances and fun.*

3. *Then, go deeper to the lessons learned and gifts that come from disappointments and perceived setbacks.*

4. *Once your list is complete, share it with those you trust and encourage them to do the same.*

5. *Celebrate all you've accomplished.*

PHOTO BY WENDY WATKINS

Appreciating yourself and all that you do feeds beautifully into Strategic Optimism. Remember to appreciate the simple things. I read once about a monk who blessed the water every time he turned on the faucet. His love and appreciation flowed as easily as the water out of the tap.

*A pessimist sees
the difficulty in
every opportunity; an
optimist sees
the opportunity in
every difficulty.*

SIR WINSTON CHURCHILL

165

Have you ever turned on the radio to a song playing that you did not like? What do you do? You change the station, until you land on a song you want to hear.

Listening to our thoughts is similar. If you don't like what you are thinking, if the thought doesn't make you feel good and in turn, doesn't support you in moving forward with inspired action, just change the thought. Last week I asked my colleague Jay how he was doing, and he said "Great!" I said, "What makes you great?" and he said, "Because I choose to be!"

Think about how much time you spend getting ready to go to work, planning a vacation, or thinking about your next meal. Do you take nearly as much time to consciously choose joy? At first, working out at the gym and flexing new muscles can be hard and uncomfortable. As you keep doing it, it becomes second nature. Deliberately deciding how you are going to feel is equivalent to starting a new exercise regime. You flex your ability to choose joy. I am not saying that you can move from depression to joy with just a choice, but you can keep choosing.

Simply *declare* that you are a conscious creator. No one comes by and makes a deposit of ideas in your mind. You put them there. Sometimes you may need a little help with that.

Let's look at another recipe from Rebecca Ewing. She knows how to stop a downward spiral and lift spirits, and she has a plan to get out of a rut. Her recipes will pull her from despair to optimism every time.

Recipe to Adjust My Attitude

Serves 1 or more

Ingredients:

> *1 box of popcorn*
>
> *1 beverage of choice*
>
> *1 ticket to a goofy, funny kid's film ala **Shrek***
>
> *1 seat in front of eight-year-old boys who cackle with glee*

Directions:

> *Exhale.*
>
> *Laugh whenever those boys laugh.*
>
> *Grin when they bounce in their seats.*

When the credits roll and the lights come up, dispose of trash, skip to the car, and take your lightened heart wherever it needs to go next.

*Note: Alternatively, this is equally delicious at a weekday matinee of something akin to **Sex & the City** or **The Divine Secrets of the Ya-Ya Sisterhood**, when it feels delightfully naughty to arrive during business hours.*

Put your attention on where you want to be and how you want to feel. If you are irritated, let yourself feel the anger, and then do your best to consciously let it go. Shift your attention to something that makes you happy. It could be as simple as loving on your pet, hugging someone you love, or writing a delicious new recipe.

Upon awakening, pay attention to your thinking. If you do not like what you hear, gently alter it to something more pleasing. It can be as simple as shifting from, "I have so much to do today, I will never get it all done" to "I have so much to do today and trust that it will all get done with ease." From there, your actions will shift, too. Remember TFAR? Thoughts, Feelings, Actions and Results are a piece of this ingredient. Add this to your recipe and, *voilá*, a burst of invigorating flavor ensues. When you clarify your optimistic intent, the lights are green and you find front-row parking. It is the positive outlook that attracts what you desire.

The recipes that follow combine a system and plan. When baking a cake, you must follow a recipe. Baking is a science, more like a system. Follow it specifically and you'll get the desired results (brownies for me, please).

Preparing marinara sauce is different. Your recipe can be more of a plan, adding more or less to taste as you move along. If you just throw anything into a pot, then you are not sure of the outcome. Sometimes it will be tasty, sometimes it won't.

A client, friend and colleague, Farra Allen, founder of LifeWorks School of Coaching, offers this:

A Recipe for Inner Joy: "Your Own Spiritual Office"

- *1/2 room, or better yet, one (1) whole room in your home*
- *One mattress or futon*
- *Pillows of all sizes and shapes*
- *Blankets to keep you nice and warm*
- *Small end table with candle on it to light, crystals, beads, incense, etc.*
- *Optional: A crystal bowl*
- *A journal with pen to script your new life; this enables you to become a "New me" and now is the time more than ever for YOU.*
- *Quiet comfortable space and low light*

Connect inside with your inner God/Goddess: place hand over heart and create relationship with your inner Spirit; make it a fit for you. Breathe deep, relax and connect with your breath. Trace behind the inhale as if it makes the sound "So" and behind the exhale as if it makes the sound "Hum." Ask specific questions to your inner guide and wait for the answers. Go to your new office in the morning, during the day if you get off track, and in the evening to take a break or rebuild your energy.

The ideal end-result of your cookbook is that it is filled with recipes that support your increased gladness, which help you to manifest all that you desire and deserve. I cannot tell you how to be happy; I can only share what has worked for me, and encourage you to produce what works for you. My wish is that you create the delicacy that you have been searching for outside of yourself, right inside your own body, mind and spirit.

Create your strategy for optimism over time, allowing the things that are most important to emerge. It takes time for cream to rise to the top; however, if you wait too long the cream will go bad. If you wait for all your ingredients to be perfect before you begin, you may lose the momentum needed to try something new.

Laura West, friend and creator of the *Joyful Business Guide* shared this about creating optimism to raise her Joy Factor:

Creating Optimism

I use rituals; they seem to come into my life spontaneously, because I am always paying attention to my energy. In my business, it is not so much about, "is this a great idea?" or "how do I figure it out or make it happen?" First, I ask, where is my energy and how do I align it with joy? The more I practice that, the easier I can shift.

I have forty-some-odd years of doing it the hard way, so my practices help me to remember ease. Almost every day I go to "Creative Bagel Time." Essentially, I line up my energy to what gives me joy. I reconnect to my purpose. I bring something inspirational to read. A lot of this is getting in alignment with my own brilliance, which can be hard sometimes.

Joy comes from expressing our gifts, and sometimes we need a reminder that the world needs them. It is very powerful to read something or write in a journal and then work on a project. I do not do any of that until I am in alignment with my positive energy.

So many times we think we should snap our fingers and expect to be joyful. When people hear Joyful Business, they think I am joyful all of the time. Yes, I tend to be optimistic, but we all have our stresses. It becomes even more important to have time where I am quiet and do what I call deep listening, to align with my best self.

Strategic Optimism is expecting and believing that things will turn out in your best interest. Here is my go-to list of things to keep me on task, on target, on plan and aspiring:

WENDY'S STRATEGY FOR OPTIMISM

1. Begin each day with gratitude and a deliberate focus on joy.
2. Spend a few minutes in quiet time, reflection and connecting with Spirit.
3. Drink a great cup of coffee.
4. Walk the dogs with Matt.

5. Make someone's day.

6. Slow down and smell the roses.

7. Exercise.

8. Eat healthy food. I believe that a cookie is healthy for the soul every now and again.

9. Read, watch and listen to inspiring and uplifting material.

10. Turn off the computers, smart phones, etc. at 8 p.m.

I do my best, and I am human—some days I forget an item or two. But when I use these ingredients, it takes less time to get back on track.

Take some time to create your plan and weave it into your recipe for optimism and joy. What's on *your* list?

What is Your Recipe for Strategic Optimism? _____

_____

_____

_____

_____

_____

_____

_____

_____

_____

_____

_____

_____

_____

_____

_____

_____

_____

_____

_____

_____

_____

_____

_____

_____

_____

_____

_____

Chapter 8

The
Cherry
on Top

PHOTO BY LEE GOSS

Chapter 8

The Cherry on Top

When we went to Grandma Ann's house, I knew there would be something delicious to eat; she was an excellent cook and superb baker. I still salivate when I think of her creamy rice pudding, fruity linzer tarts, chocolate rugelach and matzo ball soup. My senses came fully alive in her kitchen; from the buzz of lively family conversation to the taste of the goodies on the table. Did I mention the aroma? Always extraordinary. I loved her, and loved being with her.

She willingly shared her recipes, but it didn't taste quite the same if it didn't come out of her oven.

Try this one for her Creamy Rice Pudding and see what you think.

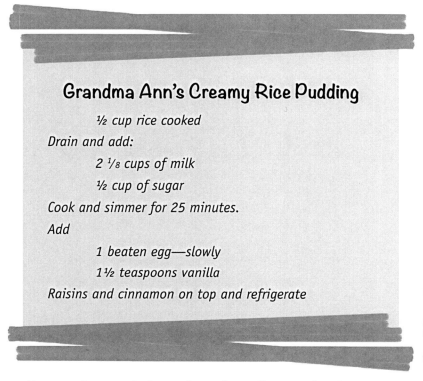

Grandma Ann's Creamy Rice Pudding

½ cup rice cooked

Drain and add:

2 ⅛ cups of milk

½ cup of sugar

Cook and simmer for 25 minutes.

Add

1 beaten egg—slowly

1½ teaspoons vanilla

Raisins and cinnamon on top and refrigerate

You now have a plethora of new ingredients and recipes. You can follow the formulas I've shared, plus create some that are particular to you. Some will be unbelievably good, and others, well, may not. Adjust your ingredients as needed.

Happiness is key to joy, rising from simple pleasures. These snippets of bliss are all around you, to recognize, collect and savor. Being pleased with what is, is a starting point for deep satisfaction. It's not about getting "stuff" and being happy; rather, the right stuff comes when you're happy. For you, it could be a new loving partner; for your sister it could be a bigger house; for your neighbor, a career change; my nephew, a new pair of sneakers. When you're content with who you are and what you have, things will come easily, and it will be enough.

Let happiness be in your best recipes.

Let happiness be in your best recipes. This is an acrostic poem that I wrote about using the Joy Factor ingredients.

HAPPY!

Help Yourself First—*Self-Care will be your Vitamin H for cheerfulness.*

Authentic Expression—*Bliss comes when you honor and share your genuine nature.*

Positive Outlook—*Choose optimism to assess your circumstances.*

Purpose—*Your passions will bring pleasure every time.*

Yippee Therapy—*My friend Robin says "Just speaking the word 'yippee' will make you smile."*

Being happy supports you in every way. If you don't get the outcome you want it won't alter your mood as much. If it does, gently shift your thoughts to something that feels better. Remember TFAR—alter your thoughts and your feelings will change. You'll feel better as you create your desire—yippee!

My commitment to write this book from a place of joy was apparent throughout the process. As it got closer to completion, my thoughts varied daily from the joyful anticipation of how much fun it's going to be to share this book with my colleagues and community, to downright fear of the process of delivering my words to the world. One night my inner critic took over and I got lost in the emotional chatter. I felt paralyzed. The only and best thing for me to do was go right to bed at 8:45 p.m. When I awoke the next day, my meditation and scripting guided me back to the reason I was sharing my passion and knowledge.

Using these ingredients will help you get unstuck, and past trying to figure out how to cook. Your cookbook guides you to sift in your passion and purpose, stir with authentic expression while taking care of yourself first. Your plan to be hopeful and confident fuels your day with energy and motivation. Your *hows* become *wows*!

When we adopted Eli, he and Abbey were instantly best pals, and Matt and I were thrilled with the addition to our family. Everything was delightful. After couple of months, though, Eli, at seventy pounds, became aggressive on our walks. I am twice his weight and

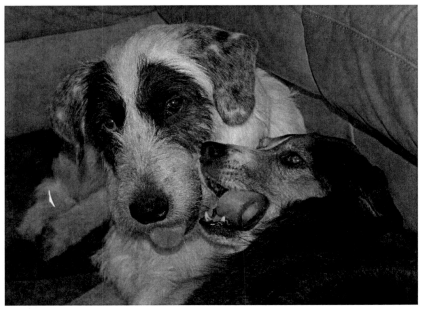

PHOTO BY PAT THOMAS

strong, yet my confidence with him around other dogs was waning, and he could tell. I was mortified when he got away from me one morning and went after a little dog. I thought we had a "bad" dog and I couldn't handle the stress.

Our hearts broke when we decided to find another home for Eli. Tears streaming, I emailed the "help me find a home" flyer. Not five minutes later, a friend telephoned and offered to help us learn to be better parents for our boy. We really wanted to keep him, and hadn't known any other option. After working with our friends and other dog professionals, we learned that Eli was not a bad dog. He lacked confidence, and sensed my fear, which fostered aggressive behavior. Today, I trust him and myself, he is sure of me and himself, and our walks together are glorious. Once again, when we let go, the right solution fell into our laps.

Do you want a WOW recipe to help let go of the need of always knowing how to make things happen? Here it is: Focus on what you want; Be happy; Invite the Universe to partner with you for the results. Okay, simple in theory, yet not always easy in practice. So consider this straightforward approach to the attraction theory and Joy Factor.

What words do you see in attraction? I make out:

Attract   Action   Traction

Attract is the first step, where you determine what it is that you want. Putting your attention on what you do not care for, will give you just that. I didn't want a mean dog, yet as long as I thought that about Eli, he acted out. Ponder the question of what your true desires are, and what would bring you satisfaction and fulfillment in your life. Do you want more money and prosperity in your life? Feel abundant. Imagine the experience of wealth. Cut out a few images of what you desire and make a vision board—look at it every day.

John Assaraf, from *The Secret*, a popular movie about the Law of Attraction, tells about moving into his new house and unpacking a vision board he had made five years earlier. The board had a picture of his dream house, the house into which he had just moved. The realization of the power of intention moved him to tears. This type of materialization begins with clarity and a mental picture.

Action is often the missing piece of the manifestation puzzle. Once you sense the essence of what you desire, it's time to get into motion. Even just baby steps towards your aspiration are essential in this WOW recipe. John didn't tell about the movements to acquire his house, but I'm sure he didn't just sit and stare at his vision board. His actions contributed to his wish. He did what brought him joy and what he loved was given to him.

Ordinary acts become inspired action, which gives you the traction you need to achieve your intent with ease. This type of activity shows up when you are aligned with your Big Why, your heart's desire. It feels different than the to-do lists with which you are familiar. When your day is filled with inspired action, you are fully alive and can easily celebrate your successes versus obsessing over what you did not complete. This perspective is life-giving versus energy-draining. Taking twenty minutes each day to train Eli could have been a chore if it wasn't aligned with our commitment to keeping our family together. Inspired action plus traction is imperative to assist in getting to your destination with delight. Without traction you are just spinning your wheels.

Attraction also includes the concept of *allowing*. Abraham-Hicks considers "allowing as the place where you are connected with your source energy." Source energy is Spirit, Universe, God, whatever word fits into your spiritual beliefs. It is the place where desire and vibration dovetail.

Cooking up something different will give the fresh taste you crave. From there, you will know which elements are best to use again and again.

Jan Stringer, author of *Attracting Perfect Customers* and *BEE-ing Attraction—What Love has to do with Business and Marketing* shares her must-have recipe staples.

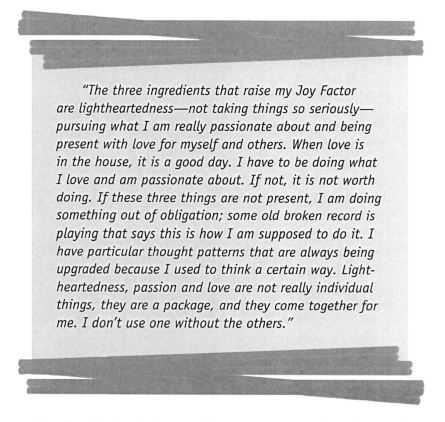

"The three ingredients that raise my Joy Factor are lightheartedness—not taking things so seriously— pursuing what I am really passionate about and being present with love for myself and others. When love is in the house, it is a good day. I have to be doing what I love and am passionate about. If not, it is not worth doing. If these three things are not present, I am doing something out of obligation; some old broken record is playing that says this is how I am supposed to do it. I have particular thought patterns that are always being upgraded because I used to think a certain way. Light- heartedness, passion and love are not really individual things, they are a package, and they come together for me. I don't use one without the others."

The Joy Factor Quiz revealed your necessary ingredients. Your combination may begin with Strategic Optimism and Authentic Expression. For some, Self-Care is the main ingredient. Connecting with your Passion will become part of each of these recipes at the perfect time. Choose one or two to begin with and see what shifts in your life. Each of the ingredients will add their own flavor and your cravings may change day-to-day.

We have a remarkable marketplace down the street from our house; Your DeKalb Farmers Market has items from all over the world. When I watch someone put a root-like vegetable or unusual fruit in their buggy I ask, "What's that and how do you use it?" Without that curiosity and courage, I wouldn't know about the inherent buttery taste of the yucca root or the natural sweetness and health benefits of juice from the young coconut.

The Joy Factor ingredients are a modest representation of things you can add to your life-enhancing process. Continue to source other aspects and qualities that will enhance your zest and zeal. Some of these ingredients and recipes will be metaphorical. Others will be literal.

Use the ingredients you know and experiment with new and unique ones to find the flavor you love. If you do not know how to do something that you want to do, ask for help.

Charles Shultz of Peanuts comics said "All you need is love. But a little chocolate now and then doesn't hurt." For me, it's dark chocolate. If it is true that a spoonful of sugar makes the medicine go down, then I assert that a taste of the Joy Factor can turn your world around. The following two recipes combine figurative and actual ingredients, to be prepared and served with love.

For Nanette Littlestone, writer, editor and lover of all things delicious, Chocolate Joy is also one of those things that bring bliss.

Chocolate Joy

Delight. Well-being. Happiness. Good fortune. These are all variations of feeling joy. I'd also like to add peace, satisfaction, and bliss.

Bliss comes to mind when I think of chocolate. Just typing the word chocolate makes my taste buds perk up. The anticipation of that first bite is tremendous, mouth-watering and exciting. And the taste . . . Oh joy! My whole being lights up with delight, then I sigh with satisfaction, then I try to prolong the taste as long as I can because, well, who wants to let go of divinity?

Not long ago I learned the secret to making truffles. Yummy little balls of creamy chocolate. Dark chocolate—my favorite kind. There's nothing better than sharing truffles with your friends. So, get a group together, get your taste buds ready, and indulge.

Ingredients:

8 oz. of semisweet or bittersweet chocolate, chopped into small pieces

1/2 C. Love

A swirl of Tender Care

1/2 C. heavy whipping cream

1 tsp. vanilla or almond extract, or 1-2 T. of your favorite liqueur (optional)

Deep breaths of Patience

1 full cup of Heartwarming Conversation

Cocoa powder, chopped nuts, or shredded coconut

1 large sprinkle of Happiness

Directions:

1. *Melt the love and chocolate with tender care in a double boiler or in the microwave.*

2. *Heat the whipping cream in a saucepan until bubbles form all around the edge. Remove from heat. Pour the cream into the chocolate through a strainer (This removes the skin).*

3. *Add flavoring (optional). Stir the cream, chocolate, and flavoring with whisk or rubber spatula until well blended. [This is ganache.] Cover with plastic wrap and refrigerate until set, about 30 minutes.*

4. *Pass the time with deep breaths of patience and heartwarming conversation. Drinks and snacks are appropriate, too.*

5. *Remove the ganache from the refrigerator and use a melon scoop or spoon to scrape across the ganache and form balls. Quickly roll between your hands to round out the shape.*

6. *Dip ball in unsweetened cocoa powder, chopped nuts, or shredded coconut. Place on a platter and repeat until done.*

7. *Sprinkle the truffles with happiness and sample with your friends. Deep sighs, oohs, and ahhs are permitted. When you're completely sated, store truffles in an airtight container in the refrigerator.*

Your joy will last for weeks.

When I "retired" from corporate America and started my company, PassionFruit, I celebrated with friends and colleagues at The Cheesecake Factory. Since I was stepping into doing things differently, this restaurant was the perfect place to have dessert first. It was fun, exciting and an out-of-the-box experience for all. Almost nine years later, I still remember the taste and creamy texture of the white chocolate raspberry cheesecake I ordered. Joy, joy, joy.

Now that you have enjoyed Nanette's truffles first, try Derek Nowatzki's casserole. His delicious take on joy and happiness is regularly shared with his friends, his kids, wife and financial services clients.

Happy Boy Casserole

1 1/2 lbs well-grounded beefs

1 cup chopped tomatoes

1 cup chopped celery

1 cup diced onion

1 pinch of cayenne pepper

1 clove of garlic

1 can of tomato paste

1 cup of water

1 16-oz can baked beans, undrained

2 cups of garbanzo beans (or any other bean, I just like typing garbanzo)

Optional to Taste

1/2 cup corn kernels, fresh or frozen

1 pinch of honey

1 4-oz package of Limburger cheese

DIRECTIONS:

It is really important in this recipe to air and ground all your beefs. Once this is done, you are well on your way to making a hearty dish of Happy Boy Casserole. In a 12-inch skillet, combine the ground beef, celery, onions, tomato, pepper and garlic. Stir frequently and cook over medium high heat until browned and vegetables are cooked. Reduce heat to low.

Optional items are to be used at your individual taste. I like corn, because the cornier the dish the more happy this boy becomes. I savor laughter. I also savor pinching my honey. And as far as the cheese goes, choose your favorite—mine is Limburger because my Gramps used to chase me and my cousins around the house with it.

It is also very important to serve this dish family-style!

Master Chef is a television show where amateurs compete for the coveted *Master Chef* title. The contestants come to the program with unique strengths and personalities. They are challenged each week to create innovative recipes with ingredients that they may or may not have used before, performing skills that they may or may not have perfected. They have only one hour to create their dish. The three judges, Gordon Ramsey, Joe Bastianich and Graham Elliot offer critique and tough love to help the promising chefs move through the competition. At the end, there is just one winner, yet all of the contestants have evolved as cooks and individuals. Don't worry; no one will judge your dishes, except you of course.

The "Burns' West" are my aunt, uncle and cousins who live in Northern California. A few years ago, the clan came east for a reunion. My favorite memory of that gathering is the night that we bought eight pints of Ben & Jerry's ice cream for our after-dinner treat. We each had a spoon and the madness of passing around all of those pints was a utopian hoot.

Choosing joy is a concept most do not embrace. People spend more time deciding on vacations, what's for dinner or what they're going to wear. Take a minute and imagine a world where everyone chooses to be happy. People would let you into traffic, hold doors open for you and smile. They would share their recipes, and maybe even their spoon.

Guess what? It starts with you. Choose bliss, and it will double like rice in the pot.

You can quote me when I say that "Gratitude is the antidote for a dreadful day." On my voicemail, after the common request of leave your name and number, I ask that callers tell me something they're grateful for. My mood always lightens when I listen.

I am grateful for the time I spent with my family today.

I feel gratitude for my healthy body.

I am grateful for the impact you make on my life. (I especially love that one.)

I appreciate the sun shining today.

Now it is time, my friends. Grab your apron, pick your ingredients and get to the kitchen with this advice from Julia Child in mind: ". . . Learn how to cook—try new recipes, learn from your mistakes, be fearless, and above all have fun!"

*If the only prayer
you ever say in
your entire life is
thank you, it will
be enough.*

MEISTER ECKHART

Writers and Artists
My Joyful Contributors

CHAPTER 1

Trish Carr: *Happy, Happy, Joy, Joy* and
The Joy in Dieting ... Really...
www.trishcarr.com
www.wpnglobal.com

Deb Cooperman: *It's a Beautiful Day ... In the Hospital*
www.debcooperman.com

Fran Asaro: *Nobody Does it Better*
www.thriveanyway.com

Bernadette Peters: *Finding Joy in the Moment*
www.citylightscafe.com

Kendra Armacost: *(Art)* www.wholebrainbrands.com

CHAPTER 2

Carolyn A. Jones: *A Simple Recipe for Creating
a Perfect Day*
www.lifeguidedesigns.com

Bernadette Peters: *Pushing through Uncomfortable to
Greater Joy*
www.citylightscafe.com

Evelyn Ballin *(Art)* www.theheartpainter.com

Pat Thomas: *(Photo)* www.photophetish.com

CHAPTER 3

Rebecca Ewing: *Recipe to Change My Life*
www.handsonhues.com

Vanessa Lowry: *Nature's Recipe for Joy*
www.connect4leverage.com

Pat Thomas: *(Photo)* www.photophetish.com

CHAPTER 4

Dr. Larry Markson: *A Recipe for Being, Doing and Having*
www.thecabinexperience.com

Roberta Coker: *Being on Purpose*
www.handdynamics.com
www.robertaacoker.com

Kay Wischkaemper: *(Art)* kwischka@gmail.com

Lee Goss Photography: *(Photo)* www.lgossphotos.com

Vanessa Lowry: *(Art)* www.connect4leverage.com

Pat Thomas: *(Photo)* www.photophetish.com

CHAPTER 5

Fran Asaro: *Make It Up as We Go Along*
www.thriveanyway.com

Erica Burns: *Ode to Joy and Open Hearts*
and *Open Minds*
ericaburns1@gmail.com

Sandra Kellim: *He Was That Guy*
www.wdaly.com

Bernadette Peters: *What Does it Really Mean to be Authentic?* and *Scripting for Joy*
www.citylightscafe.com

Julia Murchison: *Awesome Friends*
juliamurchison@gmail.com

Rebecca Thurman: *(Art)* catwoman30307@yahoo.com

Emily Lovvorn: *(Art)* emmyshealov@comcast.net

Oana Hogrefe Photography: *(Photo)*
www.shutterview.com

CHAPTER 6

Juliette Mansour: *Inner Killjoy* and *Changing the Background Music*
www.casadresden.com

Kim Nelson: *Recipe for Joy*

Chris Attwood: www.thepassiontest.com

Maryel Tomter: *Instant Morning Brew*
mtomter@gmail.com

Pat Thomas: *(Photo)* www.photophetish.com

CHAPTER 7

Susan Powell: *Wonder-Bread*
www.susanpowell.weebly.com

Tricia Molloy: *Reflect on Success*
www.triciamolloy.com

Rebecca Ewing: *Recipe to Adjust My Attitude*
www.handsonhues.com

Farra Allen: *A Recipe for Inner Joy: "Your Own Spiritual Office"*
www.lifeworksschoolofcoaching.com

Laura West: *Creating Optimism*
www.joyfulbusiness.com

CHAPTER 8

Jan Stringer: www.perfectcustomer.com

Nanette Littlestone: *Chocolate Joy*
www.wordsofpassion.com

Derek Nowatzki: *Happy Boy Casserole*
derek@amsservices.biz

Pat Thomas: *(Photo)* www.photophetish.com

Lee Goss Photography: *(Photo)* www.lgossphotos.com

For Your Delicious Life

Resources

CHAPTER 1

Napoleon Hill: *Think and Grow Rich*

Bob Doyle: *Wealth Beyond Reason* and
*Follow Your Passion, Find Your Power: Everything You
Need to Know about the Law of Attraction*
www.wealthbeyondreason.com

Tricia Molloy: *Divine Wisdom at Work: 10 Universal
Principles for Enlightened Entrepreneurs*
www.workingwithwisdom.com

T. Harv Eker: *Secrets of the Millionaire Mind*
www.peakpotentials.com

Louise Hay: *I Can Do It Calendar*
www.louisehay.com

CHAPTER 4

Sonia Choquette: *Creating Your Heart's Desire*
www.soniachoquette.com

Chris Attwood and Janet Bray Attwood: *The Passion Test*
www.enlightenedalliances.com

Marianne Williamson: *A Return to Love: Reflections on
the Principles of "A Course in Miracles"*
www.marianne.com

CHAPTER 5

Louise Hay: *You Can Heal Your Life*
www.louisehay.com

Abraham-Hicks:
www.abraham-hicks.com

Michelle Prince: *Winning in Life Now*
www.winninginlifenow.com

International Coaching Federation
www.coachfederation.org

Robert Holden: *Happiness Now*
www.robertholden.org

Joyce Rennolds: www.joycerennolds.com

Don Miguel Ruiz: *The Four Agreements: A Practical Guide to Personal Freedom (A Toltec Wisdom Book)*
www.miguelruiz.com

CHAPTER 6

Mike Dooley: www.tut.com

Lucid Living: www.lucidliving.net

Abraham-Hicks: *Ask and It is Given*
www.abraham-hicks.com

Chris Attwood and Janet Bray Attwood: *The Passion Test*
www.thepassiontest.com

Char Margolis: *Discover Your Inner Wisdom: Using Intuition, Logic, and Common Sense to Make Your Best Choices*
http://char.net

CHAPTER 7

Marci Shimoff: *Happy for No Reason: 7 Steps to Being Happy from the Inside Out*
www.happyfornoreason.com

Deborah Norville: *Thank You Power*
http://dnorville.com

Sarah Ban Breathnach: *Simple Abundance—A Daybook of Comfort and Joy*
www.simpleabundance.com

Laura West: www.joyfulbusiness.com

CHAPTER 8

John Assaraf: www.johnassaraf.com

Jan Stringer: *Attracting Perfect Customers* and *BEE-ing Attraction—What Love has to do with Business and Marketing*
www.perfectcustomer.com

Vanessa Lowry: *30 Days of Gratitude*
www.daysofgratitude.com

*Think about how much
time you spend getting
ready to go to work,
planning a vacation,
or thinking about your
next meal. Do you take
nearly as much time to
consciously choose joy?*

WENDY WATKINS

About Wendy

Who is She?

Wendy Watkins, CPCC, PCC is a pioneer in the Happiness Revolution. As a business coach, her vision is for everyone to have a profession that is in alignment with their passions and purpose, thus allowing them to experience a sustainable version of success and a joy filled life.

As a seasoned business leader with twenty four years of experience, Wendy is the coach of choice for those who desire to amplify their clarity, focus and positivity to increase their productivity, fulfillment and success.

In 2001, Wendy became a Certified Professional Co-Active Coach and received her accreditation from the International Coaching Federation in 2003. She is a Certified Strategic Attraction Coach and Passion Test Facilitator. Her Mind Body & Business approach provides a strong foundation for entrepreneurs to reach their personal and professional goals. She is a catalyst for clients who aspire to achieve extraordinary results.

When she is not coaching or speaking or satisfying her craving to volunteer in her community, she's spending time with her husband Matt and their four-legged kids Abbey Road and Eli, riding her bicycle, or enjoying something delicious with friends and family.

Wendy offers unique workshops and keynotes that engage participants in the process of working on themselves to achieve greater joy, passion and purpose in their lives and work place. Her programs have helped hundreds of people shift their way of thinking, tap into their passions and create the life they want to live.

Whether you are looking for a presenter to :

- Teach your organization how to increase positivity to be more successful
- Deliver a memorable presentation to inspire at your next conference
- Strategize, coach and guide you towards a fulfilling and successful life

Wendy is your woman.

If your meeting is one day or one hour, she'll enhance the culture of your organization with her authentic and refreshing take on personal and professional development. Partner this with an ongoing coaching relationship with Wendy and your organization will be transformed by this time next year.

Learn more about Wendy's approach and delicious offering today by visiting **www.WendyWatkins.com**.